INVITATION
to the
IVIES

BY
ARVIN VOHRA
&
CHELSEY SNYDER-SINGH

Copyright © 2022 by Arvin Vohra and Chelsey Snyder-Singh

All rights reserved. No part of this book may be reproduced or used in any manner without the prior written permission of the copyright owner, except for the use of brief quotations in a book review.

ISBN: 978-0-9992711-7-9

Library of Congress Number: 2022950152

Edited by Chelsey Snyder-Singh

Cover art and layout by Burning House Art & Design

Published by Roland Media Distribution
www.RMDGlobal.net

To Alan Turing, who cracked another evil code.

CONTENTS

1. Introduction	7
2. The Four Pillars: Building your College Strategy Resume	11
3. Rarity and Completeness	34
4. The Three Archetypes	64
5. The Three Rhetorical Techniques	135
6. Writing the Actual Essays	196
7. An Advanced Technique	236
8. Logistics and Timelines	250
About the Authors	269

1

INTRODUCTION

If you're reading this, you're probably more ambitious than most people your age. You do well academically because you work hard and don't make excuses. You've always been willing to work harder than other people your age. That's why you get higher grades. You're willing to work even harder to get into an Ivy League college.

But there's a problem. In school classes, you know exactly what to work on to reach the top. You have textbooks, study guides, and your own notes. You know that if you learn all the material and practice harder than other kids, you're going to get higher grades.

When it comes to getting into Ivy League colleges, you don't know exactly what to work at. You have the sense that "more" is probably better than "less." For example, more activities and higher grades are probably better than fewer activities and lower grades.

But you also know there's more to the story. You've probably heard of people with high grades and SAT scores and tons of activities getting rejected from Ivies, while others with lower grades and fewer activities got in.

There's no clear set of rules or guidelines that Ivy admissions officers follow. Admissions officers freely admit that they rely heavily on gut instinct and intuition. If an application "gives them a good feeling," if they just like the applicant, that person has a higher chance of getting in.

Learning the rules underlying those intuitions can help you strategically shape your application and get in.

When a customer buys one of many competing products, he relies on intuition. He chooses a particular type of toothpaste, for example, based on gut instinct. He may read the ingredients as part of that decision-making process, but when twenty different toothpastes have basically the same ingredients, he's relying on something other than analytical logic.

When people vote, they also rely heavily on intuition. Most people go to the polls knowing which presidential or gubernatorial candidate has earned their support. But when it comes to voting for state delegates or school board members, intuition has a lot to do with it. At the polls, people read candidate statements, see which statement gives them the right "vibe," and vote for that person.

In college admissions, admissions officers read your application essays and decide if you get their vote.

In each of these situations, the customer makes the decision based on intuition. But the seller has a whole different view of the process. For example, toothpaste sellers have analyzed consumer psychology and preferences thoroughly. While the consumer may feel like he's acting based on intuition, the seller has analyzed, studied, predicted, and influenced his behavior. The consumer feels emotions; the seller sees formulas. The consumer has an experience; the seller has analyzed and shaped that experience far in advance.

You can do the same thing to college admissions officers. You can learn formulas that shape their intuition. You can learn the equations that give them the right gut instincts.

Over the last 20 years, we have cracked the hidden code of Ivy admissions bit by bit. We've helped students get into top tier Ivies, including Harvard, Princeton, and Yale. We've helped students get into elite schools like Stanford and MIT. We've also helped quite a few students create "mathematically impossible" applications. Their high schools said that they had no mathematical chance of getting into the college of their dreams (based on their grades and SAT scores), and we helped them get in anyway.

This book is about learning the psychological tools to impact the intuition of Ivy admissions officers. It is a book on psychological influence and analytical marketing. We will apply these principles to the extracurriculars you choose, the essays you write, the interviews you give. You'll use these tools to influence your teachers and secure great recommendation letters.

At the beginning of this chapter, we pointed out that you aren't like most kids your age. Most kids your age are lazy, undisciplined, and unambitious. You're the opposite. You're hard-working, ambitious, and highly disciplined.

But while you aren't like most kids your age, you are like almost every applicant to Harvard, Princeton, Yale, etc. Almost every Ivy applicant is hard-working, ambitious, and disciplined. 95% of them are going to get rejected. Harvard, Princeton, and Yale admit only around 5% of applicants.

The tools in this book are going to help you beat other highly ambitious students and get in.

A FEW DISCLAIMERS

1. There are no guarantees in Ivy Strategy. This book contains the best information and analysis we have and is based on extensive research involving our own students as well as other students. However, it does not guarantee any particular result.
2. This book contains unedited quotes from famous and influential people. Some of those quotes contain profanity. We have left those quotes in their original forms because we believe that they convey the relevant psychological principles better than censored versions.
3. Many of the techniques in this book require multiple years to complete. We recommend starting this process in 9th grade or earlier.

2

THE FOUR PILLARS: BUILDING YOUR COLLEGE STRATEGY RESUME

In this chapter, you'll learn about the Four Pillars: four extracurricular activities that you'll use to stand out and get in. The Four Pillars are an Activity for Fun, Activity for Service, Intellectual Pursuit for Fun, and Intellectual Mission Statement. This chapter introduces them, and subsequent chapters will show you how to develop them in ways that will help you surpass your competitors and get into Ivies.

The best way to create strategic extracurriculars that work is to use an "essay-forward" approach. Here's what that looks like:

1. First, you look at all the essay questions on the applications for every college you hope to get into. Ideally, you do this in 9th grade or earlier. Note that most of these essay questions have been the same for decades; you don't have to wait until 12th grade to find what the questions will be.
2. Next, you create projects and extracurriculars that will help you answer them. We call those projects, the "Four Pillars."
3. Then, you write amazing essays and get accepted.

Most people do the opposite. Here's what they do instead:

1. They don't look at any essays at all. Instead, they take their best guess about which extracurriculars to do.
2. In 12th grade, they realize that the extracurriculars they did do not match the essay questions at all.
3. They freak out.
4. They try to somehow make their extracurriculars fit the essay topics, using a combination of mental gymnastics and lying.
5. The admissions officers easily see through that ploy, and those students get rejected, along with 95% of other highly ambitious and motivated applicants.

But why don't normal extracurriculars help you answer the essay questions? Mostly, it's because the essay questions are completely, utterly, ludicrously insane. Let's take a look at the first group of crazy questions you'll find on Ivy applications:

- **Brown:** Brown students care deeply about their work and the world around them. Students find contentment, satisfaction, and meaning in daily interactions and major discoveries. Whether big or small, mundane or spectacular, tell us about something that brings you joy.
- **Columbia:** In Columbia's admissions process, we value who you are as a unique individual, distinct from your goals and achievements. In the last words of this writing supplement, we would like you to reflect on a source of happiness. Help us get to know you further by describing the first thing that comes to mind when you consider what simply brings you joy.
- **Princeton:** What brings you joy?

- **MIT:** We know you lead a busy life, full of activities, many of which are required of you. Tell us about something you do simply for the pleasure of it.

At this point, you're probably thinking something like:

"Are you kidding me?! I spend every waking hour in mandatory school, sports, and homework. I'm sleep deprived. I spend weekends doing more sports, mandatory volunteering, and other obligations. How on earth could I possibly have time for JOY???"

And your response is fair. Most competitive students don't have time for joy. But guess what? That's actually good news. Your competition has no time for joy either. That means if you create an amazing, unexpected, fascinating activity you do just for fun, you will start out with a massive advantage over your competitors.

Some of your competitors will tell obvious lies, like "For fun, I love to volunteer at a nursing home." Others will tell counterproductive truths, like, "For fun, I play video games." Those are the kinds of useless answers your competition will give; coming up with better answers will help you stand out and get in.

To answer these types of questions, you're going to need an Activity for Fun.

THE ACTIVITY FOR FUN

The first of the Four Pillars is the Activity for Fun, and it's used to answer questions like the ones listed above. Having a good Activity for Fun is going to give you a huge head start over your competition. In this book, you'll learn how to make your Activity for Fun amazing and unforgettable.

Your activity for fun should meet the following criteria:

1. It should be purely for fun (obviously).
2. It should involve ongoing experimentation that could last a lifetime.
3. No one you have ever met or ever heard of should be doing the same thing.

Here are a few examples of famous Activities for Fun that people have done. Since they've been done, these specific ones won't work anymore. Once an Activity for Fun has been done by someone, it's value plummets. But this list can give you ideas. Here's the list:

- Making Tulip Tea.
- Using AI to create comic strips.
- Making watercolor art from spilled coffee.
- Making vibrantly colored crazy pastas from scratch.
- Creating high heels out of thrifted cables.
- Redrawing modern logos as medieval illustrations.
- Creating a company that sells Christmas trees and then takes them back and replants them at the end of the season, only to return it to the same customer the next year.

Here are more general categories that might give you ideas.

- Write songs and put together an album in a unique or unexpected way.

- Create an independent film or documentary on a topic that no one else has explored deeply.
- Run part of a political campaign and bring in new and unexpected directions.
- Create a special event in your city or state that is different from anything done before.
- Develop a computer program or phone app that is unexpected and unique.

And finally, here are a couple from actual successful college applications. Some of these are from "mathematically impossible" applications. The student's high school said that he had no mathematical chance of getting in, and he got in anyway:

- The creation of a small business selling origami earrings.
- The creation of a new kind of soft drink company.
- The creation of card games based on weird historical events.

A good Activity for Fun starts you out with a huge lead over your sleep-deprived, overworked, stressed out competition. Many of your competitors will discover in 12th grade that most of the miserable and boring activities they did won't help them on their application at all. On the other hand, you'll have an amazing and enjoyable Activity for Fun that will help you write these "joy" essays, wow the admissions officers, and get in.

At this point, you may be feeling unsure, confused, and overwhelmed. You might have no idea how on earth to come up with an Activity for Fun. Don't worry. This book will show you how to develop an amazing Activity for Fun. Developing this activity is a process that takes several stages. You'll go through them in this book and become an expert at creating compelling Activities for Fun.

THE ACTIVITY FOR SERVICE

Let's look at the next group of questions. These aren't quite as ludicrous as asking stressed out, overworked teenagers what they do for "joy." In fact, they are exactly the questions you expect from the Ivy League and top 20 schools.

Here are a few examples:

- **Dartmouth:** Labor leader and civil rights activist Dolores Huerta recommended a life of purpose. "We must use our lives to make the world a better place to live, not just to acquire things," she said. "That is what we are put on the earth for." In what ways do you hope to make—or are you making—an impact?
- **Princeton:** Princeton has a longstanding commitment to service and civic engagement. Tell us how your story intersects (or will intersect) with these ideals.
- **Tufts:** Where are you on your journey of engaging with or fighting for social justice?
- **MIT:** MIT brings people with diverse backgrounds and experiences together to better the lives of others. Our students work to improve their communities in different ways, from tackling the world's biggest challenges to being a good friend. Describe one way you have collaborated with people who are different from you to contribute to your community.
- **UC:** What have you done to make your school or your community a better place?

To answer these questions, you'll need a powerful and unique Activity for Service. The Activity for Service is the second of the Four Pillars.

It is usually much harder to create a great Activity for Service than a great Activity for Fun because the competition is tougher. Most of your competition is doing nothing at all for fun, so beating them in that area is easy. Every competitor is doing an Activity for Service, so standing out is tougher.

Some of the most common ones include creating tutoring organizations or businesses, volunteering at nursing homes, participating in Relay for Life, creating nonprofits that serve common targets (the homeless, orphans, the elderly, veterans), working on food drives, working to increase awareness in healthcare related areas, etc.

These are all great and positive things to do, but they fail strategically because they are just too common among highly ambitious students. You might be the only student in your school who has started a nonprofit tutoring program in your city. But you won't be the only person applying to Harvard or MIT who has done that.

Creating an exception Activity for Service that is completely unique will be a necessary component of your college strategy.

Here are our criteria for creating strong Activities for Service:

- It should involve ongoing experimentation that could last a lifetime.
- No one you have ever met or ever heard of should be doing the same thing.
- Your Activity for Service must clearly serve one specific person or one clearly defined group of people. This allows you to use the Activity for Service to address the questions that ask how you served a specific community.

Many students get tripped up on this last point because their Activities for Service involve something big like saving the planet. Many environmentally focused activities falter here because they aren't clearly serving any specific community.

Fortunately, with adequate planning, this is easy to address. You can make an environmentally focused activity that disproportionately helps a specific group, region, or subculture. It might help farmers in western Peru, for example.

Here is a list of great Activities for Service that might give you ideas. Use these as starting points, not as final answers. Any specific Activity for Service that has been done before won't work anymore. You'll need to come up with something completely unique to you.

- Weighted blanket cleaning device (to benefit autistic kids and their parents)
- Recovering lost art styles of a particular culture
- Creating a video game that gets people to take their cancer medication
- Using t-shirts and tattoo designs to preserve an endangered language
- Creating new methods of engagement for the deaf-blind community
- Creating new tools to allow those those with physical disabilities to play specific musical instruments.

THE INTELLECTUAL PURSUIT FOR FUN

The next group of questions ask you about intellectual pursuits you do just for fun. These aren't activities, but rather intellectual areas you explore, think about, debate, wonder about, etc. Here are a few example questions:

- **Yale:** Tell us about a topic or idea that excites you and is related to one or more academic areas you selected [as a major]. Why are you drawn to it?
- **Dartmouth:** Dr. Seuss, aka Theodor Geisel of Dartmouth's Class of 1925, wrote, "Think and wonder. Wonder and think." What do you wonder and think about?
- **Stanford:** The Stanford community is deeply curious and driven to learn in and out of the classroom. Reflect on an idea or experience that makes you genuinely excited about learning.
- **Tufts:** It's cool to love learning. What excites your intellectual curiosity

Again, the great news about here is that much of your competition won't be able to answer these questions. Just as they can't effectively answer the Activity for Fun questions, they can't answer Intellectual Pursuit for Fun questions. Just as they don't have time for joy, they certainly don't have time to wonder about and explore knowledge outside of school. They're trying to get higher grades, SAT scores, and AP scores. They don't have time for intellectual curiosity.

That means that if you create an interesting and unique Intellectual Pursuit for Fun, you'll be light years ahead of your competition. Here are a few examples:

Here are a few examples of an Intellectual Pursuit for Fun:

- Becoming the world's leading expert on umbrellas.
- Becoming the world's leading expert on fake plants.

- Becoming the world's leading expert on the color yellow.
- Creating a theory on how musical instruments impacted gender hierarchies.
- Coming up with a unique theory on how weather impacted religion.
- Coming up with a unique theory on how literature impacted farming practices in Europe.

You'll notice that these topics are both tiny and specific. Big, popular, grandiose topics don't work for this. AI isn't on the list. Neither is space mining, quantum physics, nuclear fusion, climate change, or any other topic that already has thousands of scientists working on it. Later, you'll learn that storytelling techniques and personality archetypes focus on tiny, specific, overlooked areas. For now, just keep it as a rule of thumb: the small, specific, commonly overlooked topics always beat the big flashy topics when it comes to Ivy strategy.

THE INTELLECTUAL MISSION STATEMENT

The final groups of questions consist of a mix of reasonable and completely crazy questions. You'll use an Intellectual Mission Statement to answer all three groups of questions.

Intellectual Mission Questions

- **Harvard:** Your intellectual life may extend beyond the academic requirements of your particular school. Please use the space below to list additional intellectual activities that you have not mentioned or detailed elsewhere in your application. These could include, but are not limited to, supervised or self-directed projects not done as school work, training experiences, online courses not run by your school, or summer academic or research programs not described elsewhere.
- **Yale:** You are teaching a new Yale course. What is it called?
- **Princeton:** As a research institution that also prides itself on its liberal arts curriculum, Princeton allows students to explore areas across the humanities and the arts, the natural sciences, and the social sciences. What academic areas most pique your curiosity, and how do the programs offered at Princeton suit your particular interests?
- **Amherst:** If you have engaged in significant research in the natural sciences, mathematics, computer science, social sciences or humanities that was undertaken independently of your high school curriculum, please provide a brief description of the research project.

Why This Major?

- **Carnegie Mellon:** Most students choose their intended major or area of study based on a passion or inspiration that's developed over

time – what passion or inspiration led you to choose this area of study? (This may also include the Intellectual pursuit for fun.)
- **Cornell:** College of Arts and Sciences: Students in Arts and Sciences embrace the opportunity to delve into multifaceted academic interests, embodying in 21st century terms Ezra Cornell's "any person…any study" founding vision. Tell us about the areas of study you are excited to explore, and specifically why you wish to pursue them in our College.
- **MIT:** Pick what field of study at MIT appeals to you the most right now, and tell us more about why this field of study appeals to you.

Why This College?

- **Yale:** What is it about Yale that has led you to apply?
- **Columbia:** Why are you interested in attending Columbia University? We encourage you to consider the aspect(s) that you find unique and compelling about Columbia.
- **Dartmouth:** Dartmouth celebrates the ways in which its profound sense of place informs its profound sense of purpose. As you seek admission to Dartmouth, what aspects of the College's academic program, community, or campus environment attract your interest? In short, Why Dartmouth?
- **UChicago:** How does the University of Chicago, as you know it now, satisfy your desire for a particular kind of learning, community, and future? Please address with some specificity your own wishes and how they relate to UChicago.
- **Duke:** What is your sense of Duke as a university and a community, and why do you consider it a good match for you? If there's

something in particular about our offerings that attracts you, feel free to share that as well.
- **Tufts:** Which aspects of the Tufts undergraduate experience prompt your application? In short, "Why Tufts?"
- **Columbia:** Please tell us what from your current and past experiences (either academic or personal) attracts you specifically to the areas of study that you noted in the application.
- **UPenn:** Considering the specific undergraduate school you have selected, how will you explore your intellectual and academic interests at the University of Pennsylvania?

Some of these questions are sort of reasonable. But others are just bananas. Asking "Why Yale?" leaves most students bewildered. Most students think, "That's just obvious. Great academics, prestige, etc. Why would colleges ask such an obvious question?"

For these final groups of questions, you're going to create an Intellectual Mission Statement. This is the most important of the Four Pillars, in part because it will answer so many of the essay questions you'll see (sometimes more than one essay per college). The Intellectual Mission Statement is an intellectual topic that you will explore deeply and use as the centerpiece of your application.

Intellectual Mission Statements are so important to colleges that even college professors have them. College professors don't research things like "history" or "science" generally; they focus on a highly specific area within their chosen field.

Great Intellectual Mission Statements are highly specific and infinitely explorable. You could spend a thousand years exploring the topic and still have plenty left to explore.

Your Intellectual Mission Statement must be different from those of your competitors. Among your competitors, biomedical research is oversaturated. While you might be the only person in your school studying organoids, for example, countless other Ivy applicants are studying them. The same applies to neuroscience research, which is obviously popular among smart kids obsessed with the brain.

Any big topic that is getting plenty of focus is unlikely to work, since it will be just too common. Reusable rockets, social media, women's rights issues, sustainability and saving the planet…All the issues you hear about constantly in the news are very difficult to use for this because they just won't stand out. Millions of people and billions of dollars are already focusing on those areas.

You must explore your topic deeply. How deeply? Many of our successful students write and publish books on their Intellectual Mission Statement. Others have contributed chapters to textbooks on the topic. Some have large, developed websites with a few dozen intriguing blog posts.

Through this book, you'll learn how to improve your Intellectual Mission Statement until you have something amazing. Here are a few examples of real ones from university students and college professors:

College Students:

- Black Liberation Theology (Harvard)
- Examining how the election technology industry's structure inhibits innovation from developing more reliable, accessible, and secure voting machines (Wharton)
- Electrophysiology of Plants (Duke)
- Uses of Media in Visual Culture for Social Change (Duke)
- The Folklore & Ethnomusicology of Southern Culture (Duke)

- Getting the Dreamhouse: Logics of Domination in Post 9/11 Romantic Comedy (Princeton)
- Quilombo Futurism: Translating Key Concepts in Afro-Brazilian Liberation (Princeton)
- K-pop and Islam in Turkey: The Pious Generation and the Heathen's Music (Princeton)

Duke appears so often in this list because Duke allows students to build their entire undergraduate education around a specific Intellectual Mission Statement instead of doing a traditional major.

Princeton appears so often because EVERY single Princeton undergraduate is required to write a thesis on a specific Intellectual Mission Statement.

Now let's look at a few professors' Intellectual Mission Statements. Many professors have more than one Intellectual Mission Statement, but each one is usually quite specific:

Professors:

- Examining working-class culture in Rio de Janeiro, based mostly on the analysis of homicide trial records (Harvard)
- The interplay between context-change and context-sensitivity, and the way in which the mechanisms of information structure and discourse coherence affect the resolution of semantic ambiguities (Princeton)
- A comprehensive examination of the evolutionary biology of human males (Yale)
- The history of aesthetic theory and the development and transmission of aesthetic and philosophic concepts during the Enlightenment and Romantic periods (Stanford)

Your Intellectual Mission Statement will help you answer all kinds of questions. Sometimes, the answer to a question is just the title of your Intellectual Mission Statement. For example, Yale asks what new class you would teach at Yale. To answer that, just write down your Intellectual Mission Statement.

It can also help you answer bigger questions, like questions about why you're choosing a particular major. For example, let's consider Duke's two undergraduate programs. (While Duke isn't an Ivy, it is routinely ranked above other Ivies, and is harder to get into than some Ivies.)

Duke has two undergraduate programs: Program I and Program II. Program I includes all the normal majors, like history, chemistry, biology, math, etc.

In Program II, students create an independent major around an important question or area of study. If that sounds to you like an Intellectual Mission Statement, you're 100% right.

If you're applying to Duke, you should talk about Program II. Specifically, you should talk about how you want to further explore your Intellectual Mission Statement through Program II.

Note that you should "further explore it" not "start to explore it." Nearly every Ivy admissions strategist in the country knows that targeting Program II is the obvious right choice. Thus, it's not enough to mention Program II; you must have developed your Intellectual Mission Statement more than your competition has developed theirs.

Many other colleges allow students to create an independent major. In those cases, in your application, talk about creating an independent major around your Intellectual Mission Statement.

However, some Ivies don't allow you to indicate an independent major on the application. That's not a problem at all. Just make your Intellectual Mission Statement the reason for choosing the major. For example, you might talk about how you've been researching how one indigenous Brazilian culture's understanding of social hierarchy was shaped by their natural environment. You would then say that you want to major in anthropology to further explore that mission statement.

This principle works on both STEM and humanities fields. Here are some examples of how an Intellectual Mission Statement can help you defeat your competition.

Your Competition: "I want to major in chemistry because I find chemistry fascinating, and also it is very versatile."

You: "I've been working to develop disposable cutlery that quickly degrades in the presence of specific catalysts. I want to study _____ and _____ in chemistry to further this research in ways that will help dramatically reduce landfill waste. I hope to work in the _____ lab and do research with Professor _____, whose research on _____ would help us to achieve _____."

Your Competition: "I want to major in history because I am really passionate about history and history is my favorite subject."

You: "I have been studying the evolution of conversational forms in medieval Europe, and how those changing forms led to a democratization of European society. I believe that understanding how conversational forms evolve can shed light on why different cultures evolved so differently, while also helping understand _____ in the present. I want to major in history to continue this study, and I hope to be able to research with Professor _____, whose research on _____ would help us to achieve _____."

You can do something similar to answer those questions that ask why you want to attend a particular college. Talk about your work so far on your Intellectual Mission Statement, and the specific professors you would hope to research with and learn from at that specific college. Obviously, mention the professors' Intellectual Mission Statements as well.

While your competition gives utterly useless answers that say things like, "I want to be in a medium-sized college near a vibrant city," you can use your Intellectual Mission Statement to show passion, intelligence, insightfulness, and drive. You'll explain the ways in which you want to explore your Intellectual Mission Statement at that college, and you'll be better able to stand out and get in.

The Intellectual Mission Statement is the "why" of your entire application. You should present it as the reason that you're applying.

By the way, once you get into a college, you can change your major. The Intellectual Mission Statement on your application is not binding. You can, if you want, pursue it in college. You can also use it just to get in and study something else entirely. For example, you can write on your application that you want to do an independent major that looks at the development of cultural hierarchies in a specific part of the world…and then switch to biology to do a pre-med major.

But before you do that, there's something you should know. Doing an independent and specific undergraduate major will help you get into medical school, law school, or business school too.

Medical schools are inundated with biology majors, so majoring in something highly specific and different helps you stand out and get into medical school as well. Similarly, law schools are swamped with political science majors, and business schools are flooded with economics majors. Independent majors help you stand out and get into professional schools.

In fact, a specific area of expertise helps you advance in almost every area. For example, journalist and author Derek Thompson has this advice for aspiring authors and journalists:

"...there is a paradox to scale, I think. People who want to be big sometimes think, "I have to immediately reach the largest possible audience." But in a weird way, the best way to produce things that take off is to produce small things. To become a small expert. To become the best person on the internet at understanding the application of Medicaid to minority children, or something like that.

And the reason why I think this is true I call my Tokyo example. If you go to Tokyo, you'll see there are all sorts of really, really strange shops. There'll be a shop that's only 1970's vinyl and like, 1980's whisky or something. And that doesn't make any sense if it's a shop in a Des Moines suburb, right? In a Des Moines suburb, to exist, you have to be Subway. You have to hit the mass-market immediately.

But in Tokyo, where there's 30-40 million people within a train ride of a city, then your market is 40 million. And within that 40 million, sure, there's a couple thousand people who love 1970's music and 1980's whisky. The Internet is Tokyo. The Internet allows you to be niche at scale.

Niche at scale is something that I think young people should aspire to."

Harvard is also like Tokyo; being the world's leading expert in a small niche is going to help you stand out and get in.

The Paradox of Specificity

As you develop an increasingly specific Intellectual Mission Statement, you'll find something amazing: the more specific your Intellectual Mission Statement is, the more other things apply to it!

Consider an Intellectual Mission Statement that has no specificity at all, such as "biology." To study that, you should study biology and maybe a bit of chemistry.

On the other hand, suppose your Intellectual Mission Statement is the experience of Irish Immigrants to the United States from 1910 to 1911. Even though it's much more specific, more things apply to it. Economics obviously applies. So does psychology, anthropology, and history. So does literature. Even neuroscience would apply. So would genetics. In fact, it's hard to find something that wouldn't apply.

Thus, an exploration of a highly specific area paradoxically builds breadth of knowledge.

In each of your Four Pillars, specificity obviously increases rarity. But it also helps achieve completeness. The more specific your area is, the easier it is to advance to a higher level. It's much easier to become the world's leading expert on the uses of one specific flower than to become the world's leading expert on plants.

THE FOUR PILLARS AND IVY INTERVIEWS

As part of the process of applying to an Ivy or other elite school, you will do an alumni interview. A graduate of the college will interview you and either recommend you or not. Alumni interviews are a major part of determining who gets in and who doesn't.

As much as possible, you should make the interview about your Four Pillars. Sometimes, that will be easy. For questions like "what do you do for fun?", just use your Activity for Fun. For questions like "why do you want to go to this college?", use your Intellectual Mission Statement. You might not bring up all four of the Pillars, but you should aim to talk about at least two of them.

But sometimes, the questions might not connect to your Four Pillars directly. What should you do then?

By learning one important interview principle, you can ensure that your Four Pillars make it into the interview.

The Power of Non Sequiturs

Take a look at the following conversation:

Fred: I'm hungry.

Joe: I know a Chinese restaurant that's open late.

It's easy to understand that conversation. We automatically fill in the blanks.

But what if a few literal-minded aliens were watching this conversation from their flying saucer? They might think, "How rude! Fred indicated a problem with his internal state, but Joe didn't care at all. He just bragged about his knowledge of local businesses."

Humans communicate with non sequiturs. Our responses don't directly connect to statements; listeners fill in the gaps.

In fact, humans prefer to communicate that way. Imagine if the conversations went like this instead:

Fred: I'm hungry.

Joe: If you're hungry, a common solution is to eat food. In order to eat food, you first need to obtain food. One place to obtain food is a restaurant. However, in order to do that, the restaurant must be open for business. Currently, it is late in the evening, and most restaurants are closed. However, there is one restaurant I know of that is still open. It serves Chinese food, which is a popular type of food.

Now there are no non sequiturs…but Joe seems like a robotic weirdo.

Now that you know this, you basically have a superpower for interviews. You can easily move to any topic you want. The most likely destination topics will be your Four Pillars. In the following examples, we'll pretend that "Cow Art" is your Activity for Fun or Intellectual Pursuit for Fun.

Interviewer: Tell me about your family.

WRONG: I have two parents and a younger sister.

RIGHT: I come from an artistic family, which is how I got into Cow Art.

RIGHT: I'm the odd one out in a medical family—I spend most of my time on Cow Art.

WRONG: I have two parents and a younger sister. My parents have been married for several years. Early in their marriage, they met a farmer. Much later, they saw the same farmer. He had moved from farming alfalfa to dairy farming. He mentioned that dairy farming was an art. They told me this story, and it made me think of cow art.

Long winded transitions look fake and emotionally obtuse. You don't need to connect everything together like some kind of android. Rely on the power of non sequiturs; remember that humans naturally make connections. Just jump to your point simply and directly.

In some seminars, we've invited attendees to write down any statement of fact at all. Attendees write anything from "The grass is green" to "Annapolis is the capital of Maryland," to "I have 2 cats."

Then, the presenter reads out, "I am hungry," and an attendee reads their fact. No matter how unrelated the fact is, the mind of every attendee tries to make the connection. For example:

Presenter: I am hungry.

Attendee: I have a pet dog.

The mind tries to make the connection. Is the responder suggesting that I eat the dog? Offering me dog food? Telling me his problems are bigger than mine? Suggesting that if I get a pet, I will no longer feel hunger?

Automatically, the mind searches for any connection. You don't have to spell out the connection; the listener will find one for you.

If you make the leap smoothly, the listener's mind will make up a connection. You don't need to spell out each step.

Interviewer: Where did you grow up?

RIGHT: I grew up in Virginia, which is where I discovered cow art.

At this point, the interviewer would most likely ask a question about cow art. You've moved the discussion to your Pillar. You have the home field advantage now.

A discussion that focuses on your strongest areas will obviously beat a discussion that focuses on random topics. By moving an interview to your Four Pillars via non sequiturs, you can make your interviews unforgettable.

You now have an overview of the Four Pillars. Now let's learn how to make amazing and effective Four Pillars so you can stand out and get in.

3

RARITY AND COMPLETENESS

College applications are competitive tests that use essay questions to figure out your personality. The Four Pillars (Activity for Fun, Activity for Service, Intellectual Pursuit for Fun, and Intellectual Mission Statement) help you answer those questions.

The competition level is insane. There are 35,000 high schools in America. Harvard lets in 2,000 or fewer people a year, less than 1 person in 17 high schools. Harvard's acceptance rate is below 5%, and the applicants are mostly hyper ambitious high achievers with amazing grades and test scores. Every applicant has tons of extracurriculars and community service and clubs and all that, and 95% get rejected.

To win the competition and get in over other highly ambitious students, your Four Pillars have to be better than the Four Pillars of 95% or more of highly competitive students. But what does it mean to be better?

For a Pillar to be better, it must be rarer and/or more complete. The ideal is high rarity and high completeness. But if you have more rarity, you can win the competition even if you don't have quite as much completeness.

The competition level is higher than what most people expect. For something to achieve the absolute minimum of rarity, it means that no one else in your school is doing it. There is no school club that has any rarity at all. Remember, there are many more schools than there are students admitted to Harvard. Even if one person per school is doing something, it has no rarity at all.

The completeness standards are even tougher. Completeness ranges from just having an idea and doing nothing with it (zero completeness) to becoming world famous (high completeness). Low completeness means you have thoroughly developed your project, published a website for it, and have a strong online presence for it. Moderate completeness means having significant media coverage. Thus, while rarity is tough, completeness is tougher. Most students find that going for high rarity is more reasonable than going for high completeness.

Let's understand what the different levels of rarity and completeness look like.

RARITY

Zero Rarity

Zero rarity extracurriculars are common among highly competitive students. If at least one person per high school does something, then it has zero rarity.

This would include:

- Every school club. Even the respectable clubs (Model U.N., Debate Club, Varsity Sports, Math Team, Chemistry Olympiad, Science Bowl, National Honors Society, Business Deca, Future Leaders of America, Relay for Life, etc.) have zero rarity.
- Well known and established outside of school clubs. This includes Boy Scouts, Eagle Scouts, Girl Scouts (including the Gold Award), etc.
- Common combinations of common activities. For example, combining music and community service by playing an instrument at a nursing home or Veterans' care center.
- Common cultural activities and rites of passage, such as doing an Arangetram (a kind of classical Indian dance recital plus final exam).

This list may seem shocking. If a teenager was doing all the above, many people would say, "Wow, what a great and upstanding kid! He's so much better than the average teenager who spends his time on video games and unproductive nonsense." That description is true. But getting into an Ivy isn't about being above average. It's about being world class.

There are about 1,690 active NFL players. Princeton lets in 1,600 people a year. Getting into Princeton requires a major league mindset.

Consider how many above average athletes never make it into the major leagues. Consider how many exceptional athletes never make it into the majors.

Getting into an Ivy is like getting into the major league of a sport. It's not enough to be above average; it's not close to enough. You need to stand head and shoulders above other highly ambitious, highly motivated students.

Low Rarity

Low rarity extracurriculars are self-created activities that you do completely outside of school, but they follow themes that are too common. These are better than zero rarity because they are self-motivated and not just directed by your school. However, they follow common themes and thus don't stand out. Here are a few examples:

- Creating a small business or nonprofit that provides tutoring to economically disadvantaged students.
- Creating an online portal to provide scholarship information for economically disadvantaged students.
- Creating a nonprofit that encourages women to participate in STEM fields.
- Creating a nonprofit to provide food and clothing to the homeless.

These all focus on common, predictable, expected areas. Thus, thousands of your competitors will be doing them.

For low rarity topics to work, you need high completeness, which means world fame. It's not enough to get covered in your local or national newspaper. You need to make your project a household name.

For example, Khan Academy provides education to economically disadvantaged students (and everyone else), an extremely common focus for a nonprofit. However, it is a world-famous, household name. Everyone knows about it. If you create something that famous, you will almost certainly get into an Ivy.

Moderate Rarity

Moderate rarity topics are different from common activities, but they lack a high enough level of specificity. A moderate rarity topic is usually a stepping stone to a high rarity topic.

For example, creating a board game about philosophy in general would have moderate rarity. Creating a board game about one specific philosopher's theories would have high rarity. A nonprofit that focused on gender roles in West African politics would have moderate rarity. A nonprofit that focused on gender roles in the politics of one specific, commonly ignored subculture in West Africa would have high rarity.

If you have a moderate rarity topic, you're halfway to a high rarity topic. Usually, you just need to make your topic or project much more specific, and it will have high rarity.

High Rarity

High Rarity topics are completely unlike anything anyone else is doing. They are highly specific and often overlooked topics. They are not something you would think of off the top of your head. It takes several weeks of research and brainstorming to create a high rarity topic.

Many of our students have had "mathematically impossible" applications. That means that their high schools said they had no mathematical chance of getting in based on grades and test scores, and they still got in. Every single one of those students had one or more high rarity topics.

One student created a weird kind of soft drink company. Another created a theory about gender based on a particular art form of a small subculture. Another worked to help save a dying language. Another created a game based on a specific and weird historical concept.

High rarity activities are all completely different from each other. There's no cookie cutter way to create one. However, this chapter provides general guidelines on how to create one, and future chapters will help you develop and improve them.

COMPLETENESS

Now that we've done an overview of rarity, let's look at completeness.

Zero Completeness

Zero completeness means that you have a cool idea and have done nothing with it. For example, you might say, "It would be cool to make board games designed specifically for the blind." At that point, you have an idea, but no completeness. Until you fully create such a board game, the completeness would be zero.

When developing a project, you need to consider the real likelihood that you will do the project. Many students start out with grandiose plans that involve a combination of AI, app development, quantum physics, and a bunch of other cool-seeming things. The problem is that the project is just too big to do. They end up not finishing the project, getting no mention of the project in their teacher recommendation letters, and of course no media coverage. With zero completeness, it's incredibly difficult to get into a top university.

Low Completeness

Low completeness means that you've finished your project, developed any relevant websites, social media pages, blogs, YouTube or TikTok channels, and the like. If your project involves writing a book, the book is written, complete, and for sale on Amazon. If your project involves a board game, you've made the board game, put it on your website, have it for sale, and have videos showcasing it.

If you have a high rarity topic, then low completeness is usually enough for a successful Ivy application.

Moderate Completeness

Moderate completeness means everything from the low completeness category plus media coverage. That means your project is in one or more newspapers, TV news stories, or the like. Moderate completeness is similar to Wikipedia's standards for what can be included on Wikipedia.

High Completeness

High completeness means that you have made one of your Pillars a world-famous, household name.

For example, the actor Emma Watson went to Brown University. Her extracurricular activity was theater, one of the most common extracurricular activities that exists. However, she was a world-famous actor. The high level of completeness made the activity work, despite its utter lack of rarity.

The gun control activist David Hogg's extracurricular activity was fighting for gun control. This is an extremely common extracurricular, with zero rarity. However, he was covered heavily in national and international media, worked directly on legislation, and built a massive following. He got into Harvard. His extracurricular was extremely common, but the level of completeness was high.

High completeness means extreme fame. That standard may shock many readers. How is fame a reasonable expectation of a teenager?

It isn't a reasonable expectation. No part of Ivy admissions is at all reasonable. But in this case, high completeness isn't necessary. If you have enough rarity, moderate or low completeness can work.

High Completeness and Sports

There is good news for athletes. For sports, high completeness doesn't require international fame. You just need to be recruited by the college to play for that college. The standards are still tough, but it's easier to become a recruitable soccer player than to become a world-famous actor.

In sports, anything less than recruitment level has zero completeness. Being a starter on your school's varsity team has zero completeness. Unless you're being recruited, sports don't help your application.

This is a common area of misunderstanding. If being recruited gives your application, say, a thousand extra points, shouldn't playing varsity give you at least a few hundred points? Sadly, no. Sports are the most common extracurricular; anything less than recruitment level completeness adds no strategic value to your application at all. Dozens of people per school play varsity sports; it's just too common to possibly have any effect on an application.

HOW TO INCREASE RARITY

If you have an extracurricular activity you like, it may seem that the only option is to increase the completeness. Given how much completeness is required to make common extracurriculars work, things may seem a bit hopeless.

But the good news is that you can increase the rarity of most extracurriculars and make them work.

A few years ago, we had a student who really liked poker. The problem is that poker is the most popular card game in the world. To make poker complete enough, you would have to win the World Series of Poker.

Instead of going in that direction, the student instead increased the rarity. She started by learning about different types of card games from various cultures and points in history.

At the same time, the student covered intellectual areas that could form the basis of an interesting card game. Soon, she discovered a highly interesting and specific subject in history and used that as the basis of a new card game. She created the game, had actual card packs made, had a cool website, wrote a few blog posts, and made videos about the game.

Note that her level of completeness was low: she made the game, made a website, and made a few videos. Her card game wasn't in the newspaper, which would have been moderate completeness. Her card game didn't become as famous as Cards Against Humanity, which would have been high completeness.

With high rarity and low completeness, she was able to make her extracurricular work.

Another student really enjoyed his AP World History class. He also started out with zero rarity. At least one person per school likes history, thus history has zero rarity.

To make World History have enough completeness to work, you would need to become a world-famous historian, or at the very least have your own show on the History Channel or a similarly established platform. For our student, that seemed unrealistic. So instead, the student worked on increasing rarity.

The student had found the section in his history class about dying languages particularly interesting. He hadn't realized before how many languages were dying out. Thus, instead of focusing on history generally, he focused on endangered languages. He found one specific endangered language, learned more about the culture, and created a project based on that language.

His project was in the low completeness range. He didn't have major media coverage, but he did have a good website and an intriguing project.

That student had what we call a "mathematically impossible" application. His school told him that it was mathematically impossible for him to get into his top choice college, based on his grades and SAT scores. However, with a sufficiently rare extracurricular, he stood out and got in.

Creating a high rarity extracurricular often starts out with a low rarity extracurricular. Generally, we advise students to look for uncommon versions of a common thing.

Suppose you're interested in chess. The clear problem is that chess is common. So are other similar games (like Go). So, the first step is to spend a few weeks or months learning about many lesser-known board games. Learn about different types of board games, different styles, cultural differences in board games, asymmetric games, children's games, and more.

During the process of discovering uncommon, unusual, unexpected games, you will become an expert in board games. Soon you'll know more about board games than your friends, parents, and teachers. As you develop that expertise, you will be able to discover unexpected, uncommon directions in board games. You'll learn about rare games as well as unusual techniques used to create board games.

Once you have the uncommon knowledge, you're ready to create something new and entirely your own. To do that, you might combine two topics. For example, if you become an expert in board games and an expert in indigenous musical instruments of the southern Amazon rainforest, you might create a board game inspired by what you've discovered about those musical instruments using techniques similar to a specific board game played by a specific subculture in ancient Japan.

That might seem like quite a bit of effort, and it is. Creating a highly rare extracurricular takes about as much work as a full-year AP or IB course. The difference is that all of your competitors have taken AP or IB courses, but most of them won't have a rare extracurricular. Thus, developing a sufficiently rare extracurricular will help your application much more than any AP or IB course.

HOW TO INCREASE COMPLETENESS

Moving up the scale from Zero completeness to Low completeness is both straightforward and entirely under your control. While highly rare projects vary a lot, here are some guidelines that will make almost any project more complete.

First, you must do the project. This may sound obvious, but many students don't make it that far.

If one of your projects involves making an app, you must make the app. It's not enough to have a sketch, outline, or white paper. If you're making a board game, you need to make the physical game. If your extracurricular involves writing a book, write the book. If it involves writing music, you must write the music. Even the rarest topics require that basic level of completeness.

Once the project is done, you'll need a public platform. For example, if you've written a book, that book needs to be for sale on Amazon. If you've made a board game about nematodes, that game needs to be for sale somewhere. If you're writing music, it should be on Soundcloud, Spotify, etc. If you're exploring the intersection between Incan dream interpretation and gender roles in Madagascar, you can put that on a blog.

Some students get nervous about making their work public until it's perfect. The work is never perfect, and the website never gets published. There's no such thing as a perfect website, board game, app, or blog.

Other students boldly make their work public, even when it's imperfect. The fearless group always beats the perfectionist group. Those who publish imperfect websites always beat those who are waiting for their work to be completely perfect.

Ivy Admissions favor the bold.

You may have heard that only amateurs publish imperfect work. If that's true, then Apple, Microsoft, and Google are total amateurs. Each company routinely sends out updates to their operating systems. You've probably had to update your phone or computer a few times.

The fact that they need to update their operating systems means that the previous version of the operating system was imperfect. They published imperfect work and then kept improving it.

There's no such thing as a perfect anything. If Apple had waited to perfect the iPhone before releasing it, we'd still be waiting for the first iPhone. We'd be waiting for the next thousand years.

Put your work out, improve it, update it, and put more work out. Don't hide out of fear of being imperfect. Everything that exists is imperfect.

Refusing to present your work to the world is identical to not doing the work at all. If the admissions officers can't see it, then for them it doesn't exist.

Once your project is publicly visible, get your teachers and counselors on your side. Talk to your teachers about your project. You can ask for advice, and often get useful insights. Discuss your project with your school counselors, principal, and/or headmaster. If it makes sense, you might talk about what you're doing with your school newspaper.

You will also discuss your Four Pillars on your college counselor questionnaire. This questionnaire is given during your junior or senior year. Every single one of your answers should relate to one of the Four Pillars.

These steps will get you to the minimum level of completeness for a highly rare extracurricular.

How about moving from low to moderate completeness? Moderate completeness involves establishing yourself as a national leader on a topic, but not yet a household name.

Unlike low completeness, moderate completeness is not completely under your control. You can't force the media to cover your project. You can't make people follow you on social media.

But there are a few things you can do to get the process going. Here are some tips:

Don't make waves; make tsunamis. Teenagers are often told to be meek, silent, and obedient. But those well-behaved teenagers never make history.

If you want to get media coverage or a large social media following, be bold. Speak out. Don't be afraid to say unpopular things; don't be afraid to disagree with established adults.

Consider the environmental activist Greta Thunberg. As a teenager, she spoke out against the president of the United States boldly and unflinchingly. She wasn't meek or polite about it. Through her boldness, she captured endless media and social media attention, while simultaneously pushing the views she believed in. If she had been polite and meek, no one would have ever known about her.

Practice your media skills and wait for an opportunity. Simply put, practice making videos for social media. Get used to speaking directly to camera. Figure out how to get your audio to sound good. See what makes videos work well and get a strong reaction.

At the same time, practice debating your issues. Talk about them with friends and family. Make sure to listen carefully as well. You need to know the counterarguments as well, and that means you need to listen patiently and carefully to those who disagree with you. Learn how to counter the common counterarguments.

Then, when opportunity strikes, you're practiced and ready to go.

Consider the gun control activist David Hogg. He had extensively practiced speaking and debating about gun control and other political topics. Then, there was a tragic shooting at his school. While everyone else was freaking out, he immediately got on social media, captured the attention of a grieving nation, and put himself at the forefront of a major political battle.

His social media videos during the aftermath of the school shooting weren't his first. Because he had practiced beforehand, he was ready when the moment struck.

A common way to boost your public presence is to piggyback on a larger public event. It doesn't have to be a tragedy, by the way. If a big story close to your area of expertise comes up, you will have the opportunity to use social media and traditional media to amplify your public reach…as long as you've been practicing your on-camera speaking beforehand.

Pick a fight with the biggest kid in the playground, so to speak. Find an expert in your field, and intelligently disagree with him. This will both increase your status as a public figure and demonstrate your passion. The kid who says, "I'm really interested in Egypt, trust me," might be lying. But the person who starts a debate on social media with the world's leading Egyptologist is clearly passionate about Egypt.

Go to helpareporter.com and sign up as a source. Helpareporter.com is a place that connects reporters with experts in many fields. Many of our students have gotten moderate media coverage by getting on the site.

Three times a day, you'll get an aggregate email that has questions from reporters. Most of the time, nothing will apply to you. If something is relevant, reply with your answer. Include your actual answer in your reply email. In other words, don't say, "I can answer your question." Instead say, "My answer is _____. I can be contacted for clarification or additional information." Reporters work on tight deadlines. They are more likely to use a quote they have than email back and forth with someone to get a quote.

If you have a big budget, consider working with a professional publicist. A publicist can help you get TV interviews and other major media interviews.

Testify before your city council or state legislature. This may seem like an outlandish request, but it's easier than you might think. In many states, you just have to sign up for it. Some of our students have testified on bills. Arvin (one of the authors of this book) has testified on educational legislation. He just had to write his name down to get a spot. Many of our students have testified on other topics. In most states, you just sign up.

If you're nervous about testifying, go watch the process before participating in it. It's not nearly as scary as you think. Testifying at the state or local level is not like a Senate confirmation of a Supreme Court Justice. Basically, you get 1-2 minutes to speak, you speak, and the panel says thank you. That's it.

A high-quality testimony can be a step into getting media coverage and making political connections. Legislators and their staffs are often excited to work with high schoolers on legislation. It makes the legislators look modern, vibrant, and energized.

The only reason that more legislators don't do it is that high schoolers are seen as unreliable. But if you show that you have the passion and competence to testify before the legislature, you might soon be working on initiatives that will make your application stand out.

Try to speak at local TEDx events. You might start out by watching a few events first. Once you feel ready, ask organizers if you could speak at one. Include a sample clip of a direct to camera speech, such as one you might have done on social media.

Let's look at the final level: high completeness. World fame. How on earth do you get there?

While we have met and worked with famous people, we are not ourselves world famous. Our level of completeness would be classified as "moderate." We're frequently interviewed on major media about education and college strategy. But we're not household names.

However, we have seen enough of what works and what doesn't to give a few general tips on becoming world famous.

Go where you are rarer and more in-demand. For example, the majority of acting roles are for men. But the vast majority of actors are women. Thus, there is a shortage of men and a surfeit of women in acting. It is much easier for a man to become a famous actor than for a woman to.

Similarly, the majority of politicians are adults. Almost none are kids. Thus, becoming a serious political figure is in some ways easier for a teenager than for an adult. While many students get involved in politics, very few try to become actual political public figures.

Whatever your area is, work like crazy on the fundamentals of that thing. As an example, many of the best movie and TV actors in the world are Shakespearean actors. Shakespearean acting is the best acting training in the world for one simple reason: no one understands any of the words. Thus, Shakespearean actors learn to convey meaning with tone tone and body language. They simply cannot rely on the words to convey anything at all. When they perform using normal words, they convey much more through body language and tone than non-Shakespearean actors. They work on the fundamentals of acting to become great actors.

The same is true of athletes. The best athletes work on strength, agility, coordination, flexibility, and endurance. Excellence at anything means excellence in the fundamentals.

Follow the examples and advice of other experts in that field. Many leaders in fields, particularly older ones who don't feel threatened by new competitors, are happy to share their practical, pragmatic advice on how to advance your career. For example, veteran actors routinely share audition tips.

Follow your passion, even if your passion is seen as silly. PewDiePie, who has often been the top Youtuber in the world, likes playing video games and talking about silly topics. He did both of those well and became world famous.

Here's a quick recap of the levels of completeness and rarity that work and those that don't:

	Zero Completeness	Low Completeness	Moderate Completeness	High Completeness
Zero Rarity	😭	😭	😭	😁
Low Rarity	😭	😭	😭	😁
Moderate Rarity	😭	😭	🙂	😁
High Rarity	😭	😁	😁	😁

APPLYING RARITY & COMPLETENESS TO THE FOUR PILLARS

Activity for Fun

Now let's look at how to use these principles on the Four Pillars, starting with the Activity for Fun. To make an activity for fun better, work on increasing both rarity and completeness. For example, if your Activity for Fun is listening to music, you can increase rarity by finding an unexplored sub-genre. Look at music from other countries. Learn about music that no one you know has ever heard of.

To increase completeness, start a YouTube or TikTok channel, or a blog to talk about that type of music. Try to speak at local events, such as TEDx events, about it. Consider taking the next step and writing or performing your own songs in that genre of music.

This can work with any genre of music, no matter how absurd. Consider Nathan Evans, who became an internet phenomenon and a chart-topping singer by focusing on New Zealand sea shanties from the 1900s! The specificity of his focus, combined with the fact that he had basically zero competition in that genre, helped him stand out. While everyone else was singing pop songs about love, he decided to sing about getting supply deliveries while working on a whaling ship.

Activity for Service

With an Activity for Service, increasing rarity can be a bit different. Let's start with the most common of all service types: helping the homeless. Most charities and nonprofits focus on providing food and clothing. An Activity for Service that focuses on providing food and clothing for the homeless would have a hard time standing out indeed.

To increase rarity, you need to start out by building your expertise in that area. That means you need to ask people about their problem areas and struggles. Those problem areas can be big or small, but in order for them to work, they need to be surprising. Once you have a surprising problem area that no one you know knows about, you are ready to create a rare Activity for Service.

A few years ago, Arvin met with an expert in homelessness. He said that the homeless community faces an "epidemic of entrepreneurship." Many homeless people are trying to figure out ways to start their own small businesses, unfortunately with limited success.

Arvin was completely shocked. He would have expected an epidemic of hunger, an epidemic of alcoholism, an epidemic of mental illness, or an epidemic of laziness. An epidemic of entrepreneurship? Arvin was surprised by that fact.

With that level of unusual knowledge, you now know an unusual problem. The solution might have something to do with helping potential entrepreneurs develop the skills that make small businesses succeed. That might involve talking with highly successful entrepreneurs and finding ways to present that expertise to those struggling to create something that works.

Note that addressing entrepreneurship among homeless people is pretty much the last thing anyone else is thinking about. The common view of the homeless is basically lazy people who have given up and just need to be kept alive. The view of homeless people as those willing start small businesses but needing a bit of guidance is a compelling view that can lead to a compelling extracurricular.

If you don't have unusual knowledge about your service area, then you first need to develop that knowledge. Talk to experts, to people who are struggling with the problem, to academics researching it, to legislators involved with it, to anyone who could provide guidance. Do online searches, read through online discussions in various forums, read everything you can until you have the kind of insider knowledge that would shock and surprise most people. Once you have discovered the surprising problem, then, and only then, are you ready to create an amazing Activity for Service.

One of the simplest ways to find problem areas is to just ask. Everyone has some small thing about their work that irks them, but most people never say anything. No one wants to look like a whiner. But if you ask, you'll often get interesting and surprising answers.

Another way is to observe carefully. See if you can find the moments that people in any field face setbacks, even small ones. Once you notice a problem, learn more about it.

A common error that students make is "a solution looking for a problem." In other words, rather than finding an unexpected problem and then finding a solution, they start with a solution and try to force it onto a nonexistent problem.

For example, we've often had discussions like this:

> **Student:** "I want to make an app for tennis."
> **Vohra Method:** "What issue would this app address?"
> **Student:** "Ummm…you could put scores on it, I guess."
> **Vohra Method:** "Is keeping score a current problem area?"
> **Student:** "Nah, not really. I just thought an app would be cool."

Some apps are certainly cool. But unless the app addresses an actual need or want, it will appear pointless.

Similarly, many students want to create information portals or aggregate resource lists to address a problem. For example, a student might want to create an online list of resources to help with adult literacy, or homelessness, or another social issue. But the problem is that such lists rarely if ever address the primary existing need. They end up looking out of touch and indifferent; they showcase no passion; and they fail to demonstrate any specific, surprising knowledge. In most cases, an online resource list unveils nothing more than a simple internet search would.

The key to creating a great Activity for Service is to first find an unexpected and surprising problem. An unexpected problem can lead to a great Activity for Service.

Remember that smaller is better. A nonprofit that addresses general adult literacy won't be as good as developing a single, specific tool to help adult learners with one very specific problem.

Also, Activities for Service don't have to be nonprofits. Commercial products can be more useful, show more passion, and help solve problems equally well.

Let's consider a common goal among adults: weight loss. In the United States, obesity is one of the biggest killers.

A large online list of weight loss resources that basically says, "Eat healthy food that doesn't taste good and also exercise," isn't going to address the real issues, such as motivation, the fact that healthy food sometimes tastes worse, childhood traumas, or genetics.

On the other hand, a lower calorie, healthier ice cream would help. The company Halo Top produces that, as do its competitors. If you start a for-profit business that clearly addresses a real problem, it will help your application more than a nonprofit that just vaguely talks about a problem without truly solving anything.

For that matter, an informational resource that has surprising information can also be helpful. It needs to go past summarizing the obvious and expected and move into the realm of the surprising. Consider David Zinczenko's book Eat This, Not That. Instead of telling people to eat brussels sprouts, it tells people which fast food burgers have the fewest calories, which french fries are the least unhealthy, etc. Everyone knows that raw lettuce is healthier than french fries. But most people have no idea which french fries have the fewest calories. Eat This, Not That started with an article, grew into a book, and is now a huge platform that helps people lose weight by providing unexpected and generally unknown information.

The key to these successful programs is that they started with a problem, and then figured out what would help solve that problem. They didn't start with the solution and try to force it on a nonexistent problem.

Intellectual Pursuit for Fun

Increasing the rarity of an Intellectual Pursuit for Fun is very similar to increasing the rarity of an Activity for Fun. In fact, Activities for Fun often generate related Intellectual Pursuits for Fun, and vice versa. An interest in performing a unique type of music will often lead you to learn about the history or culture that it comes from.

Remember, it's not enough to be the only person in your school interested in something. You might be the only person in your school interested in quantum mechanics, but among Harvard applicants, you'll be one of several thousand applicants with that interest. You should aim to be the only person on earth interested in the topic. And that's not as hard to do as it sounds. Most people are interested in basically the same few things. Finding something that everyone else is ignoring usually only takes a few weeks of intensive research and thought.

Increasing completeness follows the same path as increasing the completeness of your activity for fun. Create a website, blog, and YouTube or TikTok channel. People who are truly passionate usually want to share their passion with the world. More importantly, Ivies work to create intellectual communities. Someone who keeps his passion hidden within himself doesn't contribute to that community at all. Showing that you have unique interests and are willing to share them will boost your application.

Intellectual Mission Statement

Finally, let's talk about the most important piece, the Intellectual Mission Statement. This is the linchpin of your application. It should be both extremely rare and as developed as you can possibly make it. (Obviously, an Intellectual Mission is never finished; a great Intellectual Mission can be explored forever.)

To get ideas on great Intellectual Mission Statements, the best place to start is with Ivy League colleges themselves. Specifically, look at the research areas of professors in those colleges. You might be shocked at just how specific and unexpected they are.

You don't have to limit yourself to Ivies. Many top professors work at other colleges. See what their specific focal areas are and what they inspire in you.

You'll notice that top professors never generally study a topic, but rather focus on a specific sub-sub-sub-topic. That's their Intellectual Mission Statement.

Even heads of departments focus on specific areas. For example, Professor Betley, the current head of Harvard's chemistry department, runs an entire lab with the following focus:

> "The Betley group works in the field of synthetic inorganic chemistry to design new complexes capable of activating unreactive chemical bonds. We design catalysts comprised of first-row transition elements where precise control of the molecular electronic structure leads to reactivity in organometallic catalysis and small molecule activation. Using nominally high-spin complexes, we have discovered reactive iron-based catalysts for

C–H bond functionalization and polynuclear complexes capable of effecting multi-electron, small molecule activation reactions. This work relies on expertise in air-free synthesis and wide array of spectroscopic and theoretical analysis."

Fortunately, not all professors have research that is quite so hard to understand. Many have simple and inviting topics that might inspire you to come up with your own. Start by going to a college's website and looking at faculty of several departments. Find their research focal areas. You might need to go through a few dozen before you find one that you find interesting or that will work for you. You might look at these professors' home pages or read through some of their publications.

To get your own, unique Intellectual Mission Statement from these professors' work, it's often a matter of applying a specific part of their Mission Statement to a different culture, location, or time. For example, Yale professor Kirk Freudenburg studies satire in ancient Rome. Studying satire in a different country or time period could help you create your own Intellectual Mission Statement.

Professors from non-Ivies also have helpful Intellectual Mission Statements. For example, University of Michigan professor Kathryn Babayan studies emerging slave elites in seventeenth-century Isfahan. She considers the experience of slaves who had higher social status than other slaves. Transferring that idea to another area could be a powerful start to the development of a great Intellectual Mission Statement. You might begin by looking at elite members of oppressed groups in different locations and time periods.

Another way to use a professor's Intellectual Mission Statement is to simply turn it backwards and see if that gives you any inspiration. For example, Harvard professor E. Gabriella Colemen examines humor among computer hackers. Turning that backwards gives us humor among anti-tech groups (e.g., the Amish), a great starting point for an Intellectual Mission Statement.

Similarly, Yale Professor Helen Siu studies rituals in popular religion. Turning that backwards creates "the rituals of atheism," which could also be a compelling starting point.

Many professors have more than one Intellectual Mission Statement. In those cases, they study each area specifically; they don't generally focus on the entire subject.

With many professors, reading their actual writings will be more useful than just looking at their homepages. In their writings, they tend to get more specific than they do in their online bios.

For example, Princeton professor William Gleason writes:

> "Where turn-of-the-century recreation reformers envisioned play as the revivifying alternative to modern labor's assault on the self, American writers from Henry David Thoreau to Zora Neale Hurston found that vision too deeply indebted to the very system it sought to repair. The fatal flaw of play theory, these writers insisted, was its commitment to an ideology of fair play and teamwork drawn not from the spirit of the playground but from the production- and profit-minded ethos of corporate capitalism."

More simply put, once people started working in dehumanizing factories, some theorists hoped that play would bring forth people's individual humanity. However, the recreational activities created at the time were based on the corporate factory mindset and thus didn't bring forth individual humanity.

By applying this thought to other areas, we might discover an Intellectual Mission Statement. For example, we might see if something else

INVITATION TO THE IVIES

designed to inspire instead inadvertently dehumanized. How about some developments in fashion at a specific time or place that were supposed to inspire but instead dehumanized? Or how about liturgies or religious rituals (at a particular place and time) that were supposed to inspire but instead dehumanized? We could also turn the idea backwards and see if we can find things intended to dehumanize that instead inspired.

Reading the writings of professors can be tough. Many professors' publications are extremely difficult to decipher. So why bother with it at all? First, the nuanced ideas will be more helpful than any generic ideas for finding starting points for your own Intellectual Pursuit for Fun and Intellectual Mission Statement.

Second, reading at that level will improve your reading ability. It might take you a few weeks to read and understand a page when you're in 9th grade. You might need a lot of help from a parent, teacher, or tutor. Slowly, you'll get faster. By the time you take your SAT or ACT, your reading ability might be incredible, and your score will reflect that.

But the biggest advantage is that you will learn to think deeply and well, to explore the vast intellectual universe, and to develop an unparalleled education. You may have heard many people, including the authors of this book, say that it is entirely possible to get an education that is superior to an Ivy League education without ever attending college. This is a big part of how you do that.

Here's a secret most people won't tell you: It's true that ninth graders have a tough time understanding what a professor has written. But so do most college graduates. So do most Ivy League graduates for that matter. Learning to read and think at that level will set you far above the level of the intellectual elite.

You can start your better-than-Harvard education now by reading and thinking about the books and articles professors write. Then, when you apply, the fact that you truly belong there will radiate off the pages of your application, and your college interview will confirm it.

Don't rely on skimming. Instead, do the extreme opposite. When you start out, spend several days reading, thinking about, researching, and rereading a single sentence or paragraph until you deeply understand what it means.

You can choose professors at random. You can choose professors from any department. The more variety you choose, the better. Reading five professors from five different departments will usually be more beneficial than reading five professors from one department.

Some disciplines may require technical knowledge that you don't have yet. This is most common in math, physics, and computer science. If you run into that, put those on the back burner while you read the work of other professors. Professors in the humanities will also be tough to read, but there are not usually many prerequisites to understand what they're saying.

Whether you just look at summary websites or read professorial publications, expect to go through a large number of professors. To create the above examples, we went through a few dozen professors. Most didn't have what we were looking for.

To develop any ideas at all, expect to go through several dozen professors. To create an idea you like, it may take a few hundred professors.

You aren't limited to professors. Graduate and even undergraduate research might spark an idea. For that matter, ideas outside of universities entirely might spark an idea. As you start to pay more attention to unexpected and overlooked parts of human existence, you'll be surprised at just how many potential Intellectual Mission Statements there are.

Don't expect to develop a great one in a few days. It usually takes a few months to develop a great mission statement. But unlike other classes and activities that take a full year or more, a great Intellectual Mission Statement will help you get in.

During that process, you will be exposed to all kinds of interesting ideas. You'll learn to think about things in unexpected ways and get a better sense of what ideas are being explored at top universities. This will help you have better debates and discussions in other parts of your life, including discussions with the high school teachers who will write your college recommendations letters.

There's no cookie cutter way or secret formula to create an Intellectual Mission Statement. The guidelines above may help, but ultimately, creating an Intellectual Mission Statement is a gradual discovery process. If you put the research and thought into it, you'll be able to create a great one. There are literally infinite potential Intellectual Mission Statements. Only a tiny fraction of them have ever been thought about.

Pro tip: right before you make the final breakthrough into a really good Intellectual Mission Statement, you might get weirdly stuck, as if you've hit a mental wall. You should expect this. That wall is the boundary between what people are already thinking about and what no one is thinking about yet. It's the boundary between the known and the unknown, between charted territory and uncharted territory. If you get to that weird stuck point, you're probably on the edge of an amazing Intellectual Mission Statement.

Now you've learned what the Four Pillars are and the importance of increasing both rarity and completeness. You know where to focus your time, energy, resources, and research. Develop your Four Pillars and you will already be miles ahead of your competition.

The next chapters will show you how to use a few personality archetypes and storytelling methods to present your Pillars well on your application and to develop them in ways that give you the biggest advantage.

4

THE THREE ARCHETYPES

For the next several chapters, we're going to discuss how to use personality archetypes to enhance your application. These archetypes are personality profiles that frequently appear in both literature and real life. As we'll discuss, some archetypes are likeable, while others are repellant. You'll want to demonstrate the three likeable archetypes in your application and avoid their unlikable opposites.

Ivy admissions officers rely heavily on gut instinct to make the final call of who gets in and who doesn't. The good news is that those gut instincts are highly influenced by these recurring archetypes. We'll cover all three in detail, showing you how to use them in your essays and extracurriculars (Four Pillars) so you can radiate power and likability in your application.

THE HERO

In stories, why are we drawn to some characters and repelled by others? In real life, why are we repelled by some people and drawn to others?

The myth is that we like people who either share our political and cultural values or are somehow useful to us. According to this, we dislike those who have different views or provide us with no benefit.

But you've probably met people whom you liked, even though they didn't share your political views. And you've probably met people who shared your political views, but you didn't like them.

You may have had the same experience in books you've read or shows you've watched. You may have seen characters with different views from yours, but you ended up rooting for those characters.

Political alignments aren't the source of likeability, and usefulness doesn't seem to be the source either. We often like people who aren't in any way useful to us and dislike people who are.

One famous example of this is Benedict Arnold. During the American Revolution, Benedict Arnold gave American military secrets to the British. In America, he was a hated traitor. That's no surprise. He acted against the U.S.

What's interesting is that he was also detested in Britain. He was useful to the British. He helped their war effort. And yet, they despised him.

Likeability is also not based on morals. Fictional serial killers, like the protagonists of *Dexter* or the more disturbing *American Psycho*, also somehow draw support from audiences. These are people doing things we don't morally agree with, but the audience may still hope they succeed.

The people we find likable or inspiring aren't the ones who are necessarily nice or polite. Many people find Elon Musk inspiring. But that doesn't come from niceness or personability. He's been divorced repeatedly. He's blunt during interviews and answers questions with the social skills of a scientific calculator…and yet he's at the top of multiple lists of the most inspiring people in the world. He's even been TIME Magazine's person of the year.

So, what makes people inspiring in that way? What causes us to root for characters? And how can we use those principles to make sure that Ivy admissions officers root for you?

The answer involves the fundamental archetype of Ivy strategy: the Hero. Understanding this highly likeable archetype will help you shape every part of your application strategy.

First and foremost, the Hero is persistent. The Hero is insanely, ridiculously persistent.

In mystery shows, for example, the detective often gets taken off the case by the lieutenant, or fired from the police force entirely. However, that doesn't stop him from pursuing and finding the murderer.

Consider how insane that is. When a normal person gets fired from a job, he stops doing the job. But when a Heroic detective in a story gets fired, he keeps trying to solve the crime!

If a real police detective did that, by the way, he would probably go to jail. But in a Hero story, that's an expected part of Heroic Persistence.

Of course, this happens in real life as well. Mr. Beast, a top 5 YouTuber, often describes how his mom told him to stop wasting his time making YouTube videos. He kept persisting, even when his mom told him to stop. He is an incredible example of relentless persistence.

The opposite of the Hero is the Victim. (The opponent of the Hero is clearly the Villain. But the personality-opposite of the Hero is the Victim.) The role of the Victim in the story is to need to be rescued. If the Victim had a slogan, it would be, "Help me, save me, rescue me."

The Victim has no persistence. As soon as the Victim faces a challenge, he gives up. The Hero, on the other hand, embodies persistence. The Hero never gives up. Consider the character Frodo Baggins from *Lord of the Rings*. He faces wraiths, orcs, giant spiders, and the temptation of the ring, but never gives up.

You may have noticed that stories often begin with a catastrophe or big event. In screenwriting and novel writing, that catastrophe is often called "The inciting incident." Some can be quite dramatic: aliens attacking earth, Gregor Samsa waking up as a cockroach, the Queen getting kidnapped. Others can be subtler: Holden Caulfield getting expelled from school in *A Catcher in the Rye*, the main character in *Office Space* realizing he doesn't want to keep doing his job, Eminem's losing a rap battle in *8 Mile*.

When the hero faces the inciting incident, his persistence and relentlessness come forth. On the other hand, if a victim faces a similar incident, he just falls apart.

Heroic Persistence requires a few things. First, it needs to be an abnormal amount of persistence. If a normal person would give up on a task after a few hours, the Hero keeps at it for a few years.

Heroic Persistence also needs to overcome more setbacks than what a normal person could tolerate. If a normal person would give up after five setbacks, the Hero keeps going after fifty setbacks.

Heroic Persistence also needs to go against the advice of friends and advisors. Other people must tell the Hero it's time to give up, that it's already gone too far…but the Hero keeps striving.

We find Heroes inspiring. There's something magnetic about the Hero…even if they aren't socially graceful and they don't share our political views. Despite any shortcomings in social graces, Elon Musk is incredibly persistent. He simply never gives up.

On the other hand, we find Victims repellant—both in real life and in fiction. Victims have zero persistence, so they always fall apart in the face of any difficulty. They always need someone to rescue them, to bail them out again, to save them. They are so annoying that many stories don't have Victim characters at all; the presence of just one Victim can be enough to annoy an audience. Even if a Victim shares our political views, we still find him repellant.

Most people detest real life Victims. While the Hero persists against everything, the Victim can't persist against anything. They can't apply for jobs. If they somehow get a job, they can't show up on time. They can't stop drinking. They can't eat healthy food. They can't exercise. They always have an excuse for why they can't do anything other than ask for help. Family members sometimes feel obligated to help them…but no one likes them. No one finds them inspiring. No one wants them around.

The rudest Heroes are likeable and inspiring. The most polite Victims are repellent and irritating.

We find ourselves rooting for the Hero, even when his values and views are different from our own. We find ourselves annoyed and repelled by the Victim, even when his values are identical to our own.

Embodying the Hero in an Ivy Application will bring the reader to your side. On a practical level, that means your essays should show Heroic persistence—persistence that goes far beyond the sane.

Some colleges have essays specifically designed to differentiate the Hero from the Victim.

- One Common Application question asks, "The lessons we take from obstacles we encounter can be fundamental to later success. Recount a time when you faced a challenge, setback, or failure. How did it affect you, and what did you learn from the experience?"
- MIT asks, "Tell us about a significant challenge you've faced or something that didn't go according to plan that you feel comfortable sharing. How did you manage the situation?"

- Elon Musk asks his interviewees a similar question: "Tell me about the most difficult problem you worked on and how you solved it."

Each of these questions reveals whether the applicant is a Hero or a Victim. If the applicant faced multiple setbacks and failures, and kept persisting, she embodies the Hero. If the applicant faced a failure and gave up, she embodies the Victim.

If the applicant asked for help, got it, and then did what the helper recommended…then he or she is also portraying the Victim archetype. Asking for help is the domain of the Victim, not of the Hero.

While the Hero may initially ask for and get help, she must ultimately push to a level where no one can rescue her, where she can only rely on her own persistence and relentlessness.

In Ender's Game, Colonel Graff explains why teachers in the Battle School cannot help the protagonist, Ender, an elite student in the school:

> "Ender Wiggin must believe that no matter what happens, no adult will ever, ever help him in any way. He must believe, to the core of his soul, that he can only do what he and the other children work out for themselves. If he does not believe that, then he will never reach the peak of his abilities."

Ender Wiggin embodies the Hero.

Heroes persist when normal people quit. That makes them inspiring. Victims quit when normal people would persist. That makes them repellent. Embodying the Hero on your application will help bring admissions officers to your side.

The Hero isn't just persistent. The Hero is insanely, obsessively, ludicrously persistent, so persistent that everyone else tells the Hero it's time to give up on the task.

In your own essays about persistence, that should be a part of it. If you're continuing with someone's encouragement, you haven't done Heroic persistence yet. Only when you persist against the advice of others do you embody Heroic persistence.

In other words, if you're persisting on something really hard while your teachers and parents encourage you, that's normal. If you keep persisting after your parents and teachers tell you it's time to give up, that's Heroic.

Now let's talk about how to use that for essays about your Four Pillars. In this case, the general principle is the same for all Four Pillars. You must portray insane, disproportionate levels of persistence. Like a fictional detective taken off a case who keeps pursuing the bad guy anyway, your persistence level must be unreasonable, socially incorrect, and/or involve going directly against adult guidance. Let's take a look at the wrong ways your competition will do this, and the right way you will do it. We'll include both heavy handed and subtle examples.

Your Competition: With the encouragement of my parents, I do my best to set aside half an hour a week to work on pottery. Sometimes I can't, for example if I have a lot of homework or cultural or family obligations.

You: Even getting grounded for missing homework assignments because I was so obsessed with pottery didn't stop me. I started making objects out of paper, and then turned them into pottery when my sentence was up.

Your Competition: Because I was extremely passionate about understanding how isolated tribes develop forms of play, I decided to read a book about it.

You: My school turned down my independent study proposal to study play in isolated tribes, saying it wasn't serious enough. My parents were equally adamant that I study something more practical. I contacted several hundred professors to see if anyone was interested in that research.

Ultimately, I decided to do the research entirely on my own. I spoke directly to tribal representatives and asked people about the stories told by their grandparents. My book, *Play in Isolated Tribes*, is now available on Amazon and is a top 100 book in cultural anthropology.

Your Competition: Once a year, I write a fun limerick in a birthday card for my sister. This proves that I am extremely passionate about writing limericks.

You: My friends beg me to stop replying to texts in limerick form. That's not going to happen. If you text me, you're going to get a limerick. If you have a birthday, you're going to get a limerick. If I'm in class, at a wedding, or standing for the anthem, I'm writing limericks in my head. My college counselor begged me not to include any in this application. My response: <here you would include an actual limerick>.

Insane persistence is found in inspiring historical figures, literary characters, and popular songs.

Consider the legendary lyrics from The Proclaimers:

> "I would walk 500 miles and I would walk 500 more, To be the man who'd walk that thousand miles to fall down at your door."

The Proclaimers' competition, on the other hand, probably wrote something like this:

> "I wanted to walk over to meet you but it was raining and I had to go to my third cousins half-birthday party, so is it cool if we hang out on a different day?"

But persistence doesn't have to be about something as grand as love. It can be about something as basic as clapping your hands. Consider the following words from rapper Hurricane Chris in his song, "The Hand Clap":

> "They pull me out the club cuz I ain't know how to act But I ain't really trippin' We finna sneak through the back...
>
> ...They looking at me crazy cuz I bounce around the club But I keep clapping my hands like I'm tryin' to kill a bug."

Hurricane Chris's Competition, on the other hand, probably said something like:

> "I was asked to leave because I was clapping my hands. I learned my lesson, grew as a person, and now I don't clap my hands when dancing at night clubs."

Persistence is better when the opposition is powerful. The story of David and Goliath, for example, is inspiring because Goliath is so much bigger than David. Had Goliath been an inch taller than David, the story would have been less inspiring. If you can cast yourself as a persistent underdog facing a giant opponent, your story automatically becomes more inspiring. We can see that in stories, history, movies, and, of course, songs. Consider Eminem's lyrics from "Without Me":

> "So the FCC won't let me be Or let me be me, so let me see They try to shut me down on MTV But it feels so empty, without me"

His willingness to insanely, relentlessly persist against such massive opponents portrays the inspiring Hero archetype.

On the other hand, Eminem's competition probably said something like:

> "The FCC told me to make my lyrics more polite. I respectfully agreed to do so."

Whether a song is about something as big as undying love or as trivial as clapping your hands, insane persistence makes something likeable, inspiring, and engaging. Similarly, whether the topic is something as big as your Intellectual Mission Statement or as small as your Activity for Fun, insane persistence showcases the Hero and makes your application more likeable.

Let's close this section by asking the obvious question: is being persistent really more important than being smart or educated? Shouldn't colleges look at intelligence rather than persistence?

We'll let former president Calvin Coolidge answer that question. President Coolidge was a man of few words; his nickname was Silent Cal. On the rare occasion he said anything at all, everyone listened. Very rarely did he say more than a few words. But persistence is so important, that it merited a few sentences. Here's what he said:

> "Nothing in the world can take the place of persistence. Talent will not; nothing is more common than unsuccessful men with talent. Genius will not; unrewarded genius is almost a proverb. Education will not; the world is full of educated derelicts. Persistence and determination alone are omnipotent. The slogan Press On! has solved and always will solve the problems of the human race."

Ivies value Heroic persistence precisely because it is the most valuable trait a person can have. Students with Heroic persistence become alumni with legendary achievements, who both enhance the college's reputation and do great things for the world.

THE UNCHARTED

One way to differentiate the Hero and the Victim is insane persistence. But when you start writing essays around the theme of persistence, you may run into the following problems.

First, it can take a while to demonstrate insane persistence. You can do it in a 600-word essay. But it can be tough to effectively show it in a 50-word short answer.

Second, most things don't require insane persistence. In fact, most things don't allow for insane persistence. You can't show insane persistence in a school class; all you can do is study the necessary amount to get a high grade. That's not insane persistence; that's just the required level of effort.

When you face a challenge, it's not normal to go into Hero mode. The normal thing to do if you're stuck is to ask for help. The problem is that asking for help falls into the domain of the Victim, not the Hero. But refusing to get help on a normal task doesn't make you look Heroic so much as aggressively antisocial and unlikely to contribute to an intellectual community.

As it turns out, all people have an inner Hero and an inner Victim. Sometimes the inner Hero gets activated, and you go into Hero mode. Most of the time, the inner Victim gets activated and you go into Victim mode.

If you don't know how to do something, you look it up online, which is Victim mode. There's nothing inspiring about, "I didn't know when saxophones were invented, so I looked it up online and got the answer."

If that doesn't work, you probably ask an adult or expert. But still, that's not going to inspire anyone. No one is inspired by, "I didn't know what a quark was, so I asked my physics teacher, and he told me."

So, when does a person activate this inspiring, Heroic mode? Only when there is no one who can give the answer. If an expert has the answer,

INVITATION TO THE IVIES

then the only rational thing to do is ask that expert. But if there is simply no expert who knows what to do, then you have no choice but to activate your inner Hero.

This is something universal in all people. The second you step into Uncharted Territory, your inner Hero automatically activates.

This is great news because it only takes one sentence to step into Uncharted Territory, not 600 words.

If you're cold, you shiver. If you're hot, you sweat. If you're in Uncharted Territory, Hero mode activates.

Conversely, the second you step outside of Uncharted Territory, Hero mode turns off. Hero mode uses a lot of brainpower, which makes it exciting. But it also uses a lot of resources, so the human body doesn't turn it on unless it's necessary.

If there is an instruction manual, you don't need the Hero. If there is someone who can tell you exactly how to solve a problem, you don't need the Hero. If there's a YouTube video you can watch that tells you what to do, you don't need the Hero.

You need the Hero only when you're dealing with Uncharted Territory, where no one knows exactly what to do. Only when there is no map, no guidebook, no instruction manual does the Hero emerge.

The Wright Brothers engaged their inner Heroes when they figured out how to make the first plane. Renee Descartes used his inner Hero when he developed a coordinate system for graphing functions. John Locke used his inner Hero when he developed a political philosophy that rejected the Divine Right of Kings.

But a task doesn't have to be that grandiose to engage the inner Hero. As long as there are no instructions to follow, as long as you have to figure out something on your own, you will use your inner Hero.

For example, the creation of the iPhone required the Hero. But also every single small improvement since then has used the inner Hero. Each new software update uses the inner Hero. Every improvement in the user interface requires the developers to use their inner Heroes. As long as there's no one who can tell you how to solve a problem, you need the inner Hero.

The second you step into the Uncharted, the inner Hero activates and you automatically become more inspiring and likeable. A step into the Uncharted on something minor can be more inspiring than a discussion about something important but Charted.

- **Serious but Boring:** "In my first test in AP chemistry, I got a D. Over the next months, I worked hard to improve my grade. I studied extra, met with the teacher, and watched videos online. Slowly, my grade improved."
- **Unserious but Inspiring:** "I decided to find a word that rhymes with silver."

The first one is about an important topic, but it's all Charted Territory mixed with the Victim archetype. There's persistence, but it's not the insane persistence of the Hero. It's just the standard amount of work needed to complete the task.

The second one steps into Uncharted Territory. The moment a person steps into Uncharted Territory, we know that his inner Hero is activated, and he becomes more likeable and inspiring.

In the last chapter, we considered the inciting incident, the catastrophe that begins a story. Now you have a better way to understand the inciting incident: it's the event that pushes the Hero into Uncharted Territory, the place where no one has gone before.

INVITATION TO THE IVIES

The inciting incident doesn't have to be something bad. It can be something good, as long as it pushes the Hero into Uncharted Territory. As a simple illustration, romantic movies usually start with a positive inciting incident (the characters meet).

In fact, many other types of stories begin with something positive. In the minds of many, the real beginning of Harry Potter is Hagrid's simple and unforgettable line: "You're a wizard, Harry."

Discovering you have magical powers pushes you out of the normal world and into the Uncharted. What story analysts call the "inciting incident" should really be called the "Uncharted Incident."

Let's look at that Common Application question again:

> The lessons we take from obstacles we encounter can be fundamental to later success. Recount a time when you faced a challenge, setback, or failure. How did it affect you, and what did you learn from the experience?

This essay is asking you to describe something bad that pushed you into Uncharted Territory, and thus activated your inner Hero.

Now here's another Common Application prompt:

> Discuss an accomplishment, event, or realization that sparked a period of personal growth and a new understanding of yourself or others.

This essay is asking you to describe something good that pushed you into Uncharted Territory. As long as something gets the Hero into Uncharted Territory, it works as the beginning of a story.

Uncharted Territory activates the inner Hero, and thus makes a character automatically inspiring. For example, In the Harry Potter books, we find Harry Potter much more inspiring than Hermione Granger. (If you haven't read the books, Hermione is an incredibly hard-working student who does all her homework, gets the highest grades, and is the epitome of the ideal student.)

Why do we find Harry more inspiring than Hermione? Harry Potter spends the entire time in Uncharted Territory. He has no guidebook, no instruction manual. Because he's constantly in Uncharted Territory, his inner Hero is always activated. That makes him immediately more likeable and inspiring.

All original art explores Uncharted Territory. All copies are Charted Territory since they copy what the original has already charted. We find originals more inspiring. Collectors are willing to pay more for originals than for copies because originals embody the exploration of Uncharted Territory.

In nearly every facet of life, we appreciate, gravitate towards, and pay more for the embodiment of exploring Uncharted Territory. Exploration of the Uncharted fascinates nearly all humans on the planet, and it will help you attract the attention of the admissions officers reading your essays.

Let's look at a famous college essay. You'll see that the author starts out in Charted Territory, and then steps into Uncharted Territory. The second he steps into Uncharted Territory, he becomes much more inspiring and likeable. We'll consider just two paragraphs of this essay.

> "I am on Oxford Academy's Speech and Debate Team, in both the Parliamentary Debate division and the Lincoln-Douglass debate division. I write screenplays, short stories, and opinionated blogs and am a regular contributor to my school literary magazine, The Gluestick. I have accumulated over 300 community service hours that includes work at homeless shelters, libraries, and special education youth camps. I have been evaluated by the College Board and have placed within the top percentile."

So far, everything he mentions is in Charted Territory (with the possible exception of writing screenplays). The whole thing is a boring, uninspiring, laundry list of achievements that are very common among competitive students. We see that he's hard-working and disciplined, but this paragraph is still staggeringly uninspiring. Because the student is currently in Charted Territory, he is boring.

The reader isn't rooting for him at all. The reader doesn't think, "This would be an incredible person to meet!" He just thinks, "This is another boring resume." He might grudgingly read on, but he's not excited about this essay.

But now, let's look at the second paragraph:

> "But I am not any of these things. I am not a test score, nor a debater, nor a writer. I am an anti-nihilist punk rock philosopher. And I became so when I realized three things:"

The author steps into Uncharted Territory and immediately becomes likeable and inspiring. The reader wants to read more. The reader is now rooting for the author.

Notice that nothing particularly bad happened. There was no terrible problem at the beginning he needed to overcome. Nothing really happened at all. He just needed to step into Uncharted Territory.

Many students worry about their demographics. For example, wealthy students, Asian students, and students who live in competitive cities and states worry that those factors will make it impossible for them to get into Ivies.

The author of the above essay probably got into most or every school to which he applied, and here's the kicker: he's an Asian American student from Orange County, California. The demographics work against him. Asian Americans currently face the largest negative bias in college admissions, and Orange County is oversaturated with highly competitive students.

None of that matters when you embody the Hero. The Hero archetype is so powerful that it overrides political considerations and demographics.

Many students worry that because their lives haven't had any catastrophes, their essays can't be good. Students who grew up in sheltered suburbia might not have the same sad stories as those who grew up elsewhere.

But the fact is that sob story essays rarely work. They often just showcase the Victim. We've read essays about extremely negative things—terrible diseases, loss of family members—that just fell flat because they didn't involve Uncharted Territory in any way.

Only when those essays pushed into Uncharted Territory did they get good. For example, when someone's negative experience brings a new perspective, pushes them onto an unexpected path, or makes them reevaluate a deeply held assumption, the person enters Uncharted Territory.

You don't need something bad to happen to enter Uncharted Territory, and something bad happening doesn't guarantee that you will enter Uncharted Territory. Entering Uncharted Territory is an act of will, not luck.

The author of the Punk Rock Philosopher essay didn't directly describe Heroic persistence. He didn't need to. We still intuitively recognized the Hero. The second any person steps into Uncharted Territory, the inner Hero is automatically activated, and the person becomes automatically inspiring.

The Hero is defined by persistence. But he is recognized by his step into Uncharted Territory.

It takes the whole story for the Hero to showcase persistence, but we recognize the Hero within the first few pages of a story, the second he steps into Uncharted Territory. If a protagonist fails to step into Uncharted Territory, he never becomes a Hero, and the story becomes boring and unreadable.

This is good news for you. In the first sentence of your essay, you can (and obviously should) step into Uncharted Territory. You don't need to show that you're a winner or a good student or a compassionate soul. You just need to show that you've explored at least one area that no one else has.

The willingness to step into the Uncharted shows the Heroic parts of your personality far more than any achievement. According to philosopher Robert Pirsig, author of *Zen and the Art of Motorcycle Maintenance*, the most Heroic moment in the Iliad was when Hector chose to fight Achilles, knowing he had no chance of winning.

Victory does not define Heroism. The first step into Uncharted Territory makes the applicant inspiring.

Consider this: What do you do on September 3rd every year?

In the U.S., we don't do anything special on September 3rd unless it happens to fall on Labor Day. On September 3rd, we have no fireworks, special tributes, or patriotic concerts.

But we do on July 4th.

July 4th is Independence Day in the U.S., but July 4, 1776 wasn't our day of independence; it was just the day the Declaration of Independence was signed.

The American colonies became independent on September 3, 1783 when the Treaty of Paris was signed, but no one celebrates that day's success. We celebrate the day the American colonies stepped into Uncharted Territory and declared their independence.

The true Heroic moment isn't the moment of victory; it's the moment that the Hero steps into Uncharted Territory. That step into the Uncharted is magnetic, likeable, and inspiring.

When Ivies are trying to help the downtrodden or promote their own political agendas, they end up being highly influenced by the draw of the Uncharted. For example, being the first person in your family to attend college currently boosts your application. If college is Uncharted Territory for you and your family, your story becomes more appealing.

That may look like helping the downtrodden, and many Ivy admissions officers undoubtedly think it is that. But the fact is that Ivies don't try to let in the depressed, the academically struggling, the people who feel overshadowed by successful parents, people addicted to narcotics, or many people suffering with far worse things than, "My parents didn't go to college, but they gave me the best education they could."

Compare Ivies with people who focus on helping the downtrodden. Mother Theresa, for example, focused on caring for lepers, homeless youth, and the dying. I doubt Harvard is going to try to get those groups admitted any time soon.

Ivy admission policies have little to do with indiscriminately helping the downtrodden, and everything to do with being part of the stories of those stepping into Uncharted Territory. Make Uncharted Territory your North Star, and you will increase your chances of getting in.

The Hero in Your Pillars

Each of your Four Pillars should go into Uncharted Territory. The Intellectual Mission Statement may explore Uncharted Territory in a serious way. For example, you might study how learning techniques from pre-literate civilizations might help students with ADHD. On the other hand, an Activity for Fun might explore Uncharted Territory in a lighter way, such as making weird tasting candies.

Your Four Pillars don't need to achieve any goal to be inspiring and strategically effective. Merely stepping into Uncharted Territory and trying to pursue a goal is enough. It doesn't matter if you never achieve it.

However, you do need to show persistence. If you work at something Uncharted for years and try all kinds of different approaches that don't end up working, that's fine. If you try something Uncharted for a few minutes and give up, that shows a lack of persistence and ends up portraying the Victim.

The Hero must step into Uncharted Territory and then be relentlessly persistent. For each of your Four Pillars, make sure you can show that you're in Uncharted Territory and insanely persistent.

UNIVERSITIES AND THE UNCHARTED

This focus on the Uncharted begs the question: what does Unchartedness have to do with university education? Don't colleges exist to teach information that has already been charted by someone else? Isn't the ideal college student someone who is good at learning and retaining that information?

This is a common misunderstanding about colleges. The common, and incorrect, belief is that colleges are essentially advanced high schools. The reality is quite different.

Colleges exist to do research. In other words, their goal is to explore Uncharted Territory. For a professor to advance in his career, he needs to publish research. Better researchers are the ones who get tenure, not better teachers. Research is a requirement for tenure, but teaching well isn't.

So why do colleges teach at all? Why not just do research? Colleges teach to raise money for research.

Those who go to college to learn pay huge fees. Undergraduate students, medical students, business school students, and law students pay exorbitant tuitions to learn, so that professors and academic graduate students can get paid to research. Graduate students involved in research get paid to be there. (They might not get paid a lot, but it's still better than having to pay to attend.)

Teaching at universities is often done by adjunct professors, who are short term hires there to do the teaching, while the real professors focus on research.

Teaching is for a university what bake sales are for a church. Churches do bake sales to raise money for their real goals, not because they want to become bakeries. Churches routinely hire short term staff to help with bake sales, but they never hire temps to do the sermons or perform sacraments.

INVITATION TO THE IVIES

Similarly, teaching is just a way for colleges to raise money. It's often done by temps (adjuncts) or graduate students, rather than by full professors.

You may discover that teaching quality at universities varies wildly, just as the quality of baked goods varies wildly at church bake sales. Teaching isn't important to them; research is.

In your essays about why you want to attend a college, you should focus on research rather than courses. Many students will talk about specific courses in the Why This College essays, but that is unlikely to work. Instead, you should focus your thought and intentions on research.

Make your focus specific; talk about the research of one professor and how it relates to your own Intellectual Mission Statement. With a specific essay that focuses on the Uncharted, you'll easily defeat competitors who have a general focus that completely misses the point of a university.

Your Competition: I want to attend _____ because it has a world class faculty and wonderful courses in a variety of subjects. (Note that your competition's answer could apply to basically any college on earth.)

You: Professor Q's research in DNA processing in frog cells looks at the way biological data is compressed, specifically through _____. Those same methods could create a new path to rethinking digital image compression, which I have been researching for the last few years by doing _____. At Yale, I hope to research with Professor Q and work toward a type of image compression that would draw from biological data compression to reduce file size and preserve image integrity.

You may think it seems farfetched that someone would want to go to a particular college because of the research of one specific professor. And it is rare; 95% of students would never think like that. Those are the 95% who get rejected.

In fact, many famous Ivy graduates indicated that they picked their college based on one single professor. Jeffrey Eugenides, one of the most influential living novelists, chose to attend Brown based on one specific professor.

This tendency is even more common among academic graduate students. Academic graduate students are those pursuing graduate studies towards masters or doctorate degrees. They are not medical, law, or business students. Unlike undergraduate, medical, or law students, academic graduate students get paid to be there. When serious graduate students explain why they picked a particular PhD program, they routinely discuss the specific research of a specific professor.

Colleges use undergraduate student tuition to fund graduate student research. They pay graduate students, who are explorers of the Uncharted, and charge undergraduates tuition. Adopting the mindset of graduate students in small ways, such as by talking about one specific professor, can help you get in.

But the biggest way to mimic graduate students is to focus on the Uncharted. All PhD students must perform original research. Similarly, you should make your Four Pillars Uncharted, and you should focus your essays on the parts of the university that explore the Uncharted. Discuss professorial research, entrepreneurship programs (which inherently explore the Uncharted), independent studies, undergraduate research, collaborative labs, etc. Make your application entirely about the Uncharted to help yourself stand out and get in.

PRE-MED AND THE UNCHARTED

This section is only for students who are considering careers in medicine.

You may have heard college strategists advise against admitting that you're pre-med on your application. Pre-med students are among the most competitive, so being pre-med means facing tougher opponents.

Also, pre-med is the most oversaturated undergraduate program. Millions of teenagers want to be doctors. So, when you indicate pre-med, you're placing yourself directly in competition with those highly motivated STEM students. You face stiffer competition while showcasing much less scarcity.

But at the same time, you know that some pre-med kids do get into Harvard. Clearly, it can be done. While being pre-med usually doesn't work, sometimes it does. What's the secret?

You already know it. Most students see studying medicine as something like this:

1. You learn medicine.
2. You apply what you learn.
3. You get money and social status.

See the problem? Everything about that is Charted. There's not the slightest hint of Uncharted Territory there.

Actual medicine is all about Uncharted Territory. Research and innovation are constant. Even doctors who don't engage in lab research still constantly try to develop new techniques, such as new ways to interact with patients, new ways to make patients comfortable, new ways to reach out to patients, new ways to increase compliance with prescriptions.

The key to a successful pre-med application is the same as the secret to any application: the Uncharted. Talk about what small aspects of medicine you've already started exploring, and what completely new ideas you have.

Your new ideas don't have to be grandiose. You don't need to have a new cure for cancer. Your innovations can be small. It can be anything from redesigning a waiting room to working on a physical tool to help with one specific medical task.

You should discuss Uncharted elements of non-medical research as well. Make sure all Four Pillars are about the Uncharted so that Unchartedness radiates from your application.

A pre-med application is still harder than any other kind of application. Unless you're applying to a combined medical program (e.g., Brown's PLME program), there's no real reason to have an application that focuses on medicine. Remember, you can change your major after you get to college. You can say you want to pursue an independent major about the communication practices of seahorses, and then change your mind once you get in.

But keep one thing in mind: if you are applying to the PLME program, your undergraduate major should be something other than biology or chemistry. The purpose of the PLME program is to allow students to explore non-medical areas to help them become more complete physicians. If you're applying to PLME, you should discuss creating a specific independent major derived from your Intellectual Mission Statement.

INVITATION TO THE IVIES

THE UNIVERSALITY OF THE HERO

You've probably heard the saying that we hate in others what we hate in ourselves. It works the other way too: we like in others what we like in ourselves.

Most of our discussion of the likeability of the Hero is based on that. People like their inner Heroes, and thus like the inner Heroes of others.

Every single person has an inner Hero. In this chapter we will discuss how that inner Hero is created and why it is found in all people, in all cultures, at all times in history, and in all parts of the world. We'll also discuss why the Hero archetype is so powerful.

Let's start with why the Hero and Victim archetypes are so powerful. Early childhood experiences tend to have a profound influence on the psyche. The earlier the experience, the more it affects the personality. A person who got bitten by a dog at age 4 is more likely to develop a fear of dogs than someone who got bitten by a dog at age 40.

The Hero and Victim are so powerful and so universal because they are formed in infancy. You can watch them forming in an infant. You don't need any specialized psychological training; it is visible to anyone who knows what to look for.

When a baby relentlessly tries to break out of a playpen, or get into a forbidden cabinet, you see the inner Hero. The infant's inner Hero is staggeringly persistent.

To this day, we have never seen an intact playpen in anyone's home, ever. Even though playpens are made using nylon with extremely high tensile strength, somehow every infant on earth manages to break a hole through his or her playpen.

Parents must use childproof locks to keep infants and toddlers out of dangerous cabinets. Those locks are so complex that they are also basically adult proof. The only reason that adults can get past the locks is that they can read the instructions.

The inner Hero of an infant is endlessly relentless. When an infant is trying to get into a forbidden area, he just never gives up.

Now, the infant's inner Victim is also easy to spot. When a baby cries for help, that's the Victim. Babies do this all the time, obviously.

The inner Victim develops first. For the first 6 months of life, all babies can do is cry for help.

The problem-solving approach of a baby follows that same pattern. The baby always tries the Victim approach first. If that works, the Hero is never engaged.

For example, if the baby wants food, she cries. The adult gives her food. If she needs a diaper change, she cries, and the adult handles it. If she wants to be picked up, she cries, and gets picked up.

But sometimes, the inner Victim can't solve the problem. Suppose the baby wants to get into that forbidden cabinet. Maybe the cabinet contains cleaning supplies or medicines. The baby starts by crying and pointing at the forbidden cabinet. In other words, she starts out with the inner Victim. The parent obviously refuses to let the infant into that cabinet.

So, the baby amplifies the inner Victim. She cries louder, points more emphatically. But it doesn't work. The parent still won't let her into the cabinet. The baby tries this for a while, hoping that if the inner Victim has enough time to work, eventually the adult will cave.

Then, something changes. Once the baby is 100% sure that no adult will help her, the crying stops. She falls into a strategic calm. She's no longer relying on the helper adult. The inner Hero has been activated.

She's now going to wait for the adult to be distracted and then silently scurry over to the forbidden cabinet. She's going to work away at the lock. If the adult notices and moves her to another room, she'll sneak back as soon as the adult's back is turned. She'll continue this for days, weeks, months if needed.

Every person has an inner Hero and an inner Victim, created in infancy. Like the baby, when faced with a difficulty, we first try to use our inner Victim. We first ask for help. Only if there is no help to be had do we activate our inner Hero.

It also explains why we are drawn to those who embody the Hero. We all have inner Heroes. Like the inner Victim, the inner Hero is inborn. It's created in everyone in infancy.

It feels powerful, unlike the inner Victim which feels helpless. We admire our own inner Heroism, and thus we deeply admire it in others as well.

The inner Hero is the embodiment of our first independent success. That experience—succeeding without any help—creates an aspect of ourselves that we cherish. Thus, when we see it in others, we're drawn to that person.

We all need to cry for help for the first several months of life. Thus, we all develop an inner Victim. Also, all infants want to do things that adults won't help with. As far as we know, no adult on earth has helped an infant tear a hole into the side of a playpen, for example. Thus, we all need to develop the inner Hero.

These archetypes are more powerful than politics, social norms, professionalism, and nearly everything else because they were created much earlier than all those things. The Hero and Victim are the two initial poles of our existence, created in infancy.

When you're working on your Four Pillars, think about the persistence of the infant. Infants keep working away at tasks for months without relenting. You did that as an infant; you can be even more persistent now if you tap into it.

If you ask most adults if they believe they can rip a nylon rope with their bare hands, they will say no. If you change the question and ask the adult if they believe they could rip through it if they just worked away at it for six months straight without giving up (like an infant working away at a nylon playpen), most will say yes. The unstoppable persistence that you were born with is the secret to making your Four Pillars amazing.

THE ADULT HERO

The Hero is an incredibly powerful archetype. But there's one archetype more powerful, more inspiring, and more useful for an Ivy Application: the Adult Hero.

In hero myths, the Hero has a Guide. For example, Harry Potter's guide is Dumbledore. At some point in any Hero story, the Guide must either die or leave. If he leaves, he must leave permanently and in such a way that he can no longer guide the Hero. For example, he might move to a different planet.

After the Guide dies, the Hero must establish himself as an Adult Hero. How does he do this? He must reject a fundamental view held by the Guide. Once he rejects his Guide and moves in his own, new direction, he is seen as the Adult Hero, the positive evolution of the Hero.

In the final book of the Harry Potter series, for example, Harry rejects Dumbledore's principle of secrecy and independence, and instead embraces openness, trust, and collaboration. Once he does that, he transforms into the Adult Hero.

Notice that the mere death of the Guide does not transform the Hero into an Adult Hero. The Hero must reject a fundamental view of the Guide.

In fact, in some stories the Guide is dead from the beginning, but still acts as the Guide. In the Showtime series *Dexter*, for example, Dexter's father is the guide. He's dead from the beginning, but Dexter still relies on his father's rules and principles. Only when he rejects one of those principles does Dexter become an Adult Hero.

The Guide doesn't need to die for the Hero to become the Adult Hero. For example, James Bond's guide is M...but he always goes against at least one of M's critical orders. In the *Star Trek* universe, the Guide is the Prime Directive, but Captains Kirk, Picard, and Janeway all violate it multiple times.

Hero myths and the Hero Archetype are universal because they come from guaranteed experiences that every living person has. All infants develop an inner Victim because they all need to cry for help. All infants develop an inner Hero because at some point they want to do something that an adult will not help with (like making a hole in the wall of a playpen).

For a child, the parent is the usual Guide. Young children tend to have the same opinions as their parents. If the parent thinks Mercedes cars are the best, the young child agrees. If the parent is a Democrat, the young child is a Democrat. If the parent thinks hard work is the most important thing, so does the young child. Even if the child doesn't work hard, he still believes that hard work is the most important thing.

As the child becomes a teenager, things change. He can think logically and independently. Invariably, he disagrees with one parental view or another.

That action of rejecting a parental view is symbolized in the Hero myth when the Hero rejects a view of the Guide. This process of becoming an Adult Hero is universal. Thus, the Adult Hero is a universal archetype found in all civilizations and time periods. The Adult Hero is more magnetic, likeable, and inspiring than the Hero.

We all prize that independence we develop as teenagers. There is not a single person on earth who honestly wishes he could not think independently. Because we prize that independence within ourselves, we are drawn to it in others.

With the Hero, we discussed the opposite of all that persistence and Unchartedness: the Victim. The Adult Hero also has an opposite that you must actively avoid: the Villain.

Interestingly, the Villain shares many traits with the Hero. They both persevere indefinitely, never give up, and step into Uncharted Territory. This is why so many compelling stories can be written by turning the Villain from one story into the protagonist of another (Lucifer, Grendel, Cruella De Ville, the Joker, and every character in *Game of Thrones*).

But ultimately, the Hero defeats the Villain, even when the Villain appears stronger. David beat Goliath. Harry Potter defeated Voldemort. The Allies defeated the Nazis.

In college strategy, Adult Hero applications defeat Villain applications. By understanding one critical difference between the Adult Hero and the Villain, we can create applications that will help you stand out and get in.

UNIVERSAL REJECTION OR DISMISSIVENESS.

The Adult Hero rejects one critical principle of the guide. This can be seen as a pivotal disagreement, a debate that advances the morality, theory, or understanding of an issue. The Villain, on the other hand, rejects all the views of the guide. The Villain's role is to reject the Guide completely.

For example, in the Harry Potter books, Harry rejects one of Dumbledore's views to become the Adult Hero. Voldemort, on the other hand, rejects all of Dumbledore's views.

How does that look in college strategy? Suppose we've selected a professor who is researching hippopotamus communication. Our goal is to come across as the Adult Hero. To do that, we must disagree with one core idea of the professor.

Here's what the Adult Hero's answer might look like:

> "Professor H argues that hippos communicate through sound and gesture. But he overlooks one of the most important types of communication: environmental change. Just as humans communicate affection through beautifying an area with flowers or convey hatred through vandalism, animals communicate by altering their environment."

On the other hand, here's the Villain's answer:

> "Professor H argues that hippos communicate through sound and gesture. But studying hippos is just stupid and a waste of time. He should get a better hobby."

This showcases the Villain, not the Adult Hero. The answer suggests a dismissive naysayer, not a critical thinker. That example seems obviously bad, but the Villain can be more subtle. For example:

> "Professor H argues that hippos communicate through sound and gesture. But, hippos are too lumbering to gesture clearly and they don't make a lot of sound."

When students start out on the path of creating clever, insightful disagreements…they tend to fall into the Villain trap a few times. You can't just reject everything the Guide said and leave it there. You must reject an aspect of what the Guide said and offer an alternative that advances human understanding.

The Adult Hero moves the exploration of the Uncharted forward. The Villain is just an annoying pessimist. The Adult Hero engages with the topic. The Villain dismisses the topic.

Let's look at a real example from a real Duke alumni interviewer, Randy Haldeman. He posted on Quora an experience he had with a student. He had asked a standard question: "If you could meet anyone past or present, who would you meet with?" Here's what the interviewer described:

> "I even had one 'physics expert' guy answer, 'I don't want to meet anyone because there is nothing I can learn from them.' I suggested Albert Einstein to discuss his theory of relativity and the kid answered 'I'm gonna prove Einstein wrong.'
>
> By ignoring even the option to debate Einstein in person, he would not be a good fit for Duke so I rated him a 1-of-5 and he was rejected."

In this case, the student came across as the dismissive Villain instead of the engaged Adult Hero.

However, with a small change in either the question or answer, an interviewee can come across as the Adult Hero instead. For example, if a student said he wanted to disprove one specific part of Einstein's General

Theory of Relativity, that would embody the Adult Hero. Similarly, if the question had been, "If you met Einstein, what would you do?", the answer, "Prove him wrong about <something specific>," would embody the Adult Hero. In fact, for that question, even an answer like "Prove him wrong" might be interpreted as the Adult Hero instead of the Villain.

That student ended up getting into Stanford. Either the question or his response must have been different enough to be perceived as the engaged Adult Hero rather than the dismissive Villain.

The Adult Hero and Villain archetypes have enough in common that under pressure, they can easily get muddled. The key to remember is that the Adult Hero rejects only one view of the Guide, while the Villain dismisses all the views of the Guide.

To embody the Adult Hero, first engage with the topic and then reject one view of the Guide. If you preemptively reject the topic, you will embody the Villain and massively harm your chances of admission.

THE ADULT HERO AND THE FOUR PILLARS

The Adult Hero archetype can help you improve your Four Pillars. In each of your Four Pillars, you can reject one view of the Guide.

But who on earth is the Guide? If you're doing a quirky Activity for Fun, it's unlikely that a wise old man is guiding you.

Remember, we're working at the level of psychological archetypes. Thus, the Guide can be anything that provides guidance. The Guide can be a person, such as a parent, grandparent, or teacher. But it can also be the dictionary. It can also be a prevailing view.

For example, suppose that you decide to create a jelly bean company that makes spicy jelly beans instead of sweet ones. The company itself inherently and subtly rejects a view of the Guide, in this case the prevailing view that jelly beans should be sweet.

Sometimes it will look much more like a classic Hero myth. For example, your Intellectual Mission Statement might have something to do with adult literacy. You might just publicly disagree with an actual expert in the field over something she claimed. You would agree with the overall idea that improving adult literacy is good, but reject one specific view, such as the idea that multi-modal teaching is a good solution for adult learners.

The Adult Hero rejects one view of the Guide but doesn't dismiss the topic itself. In fact, the Adult Hero and the Hero both take it one step further and become "un-dismissive," allowing them to defeat the Villain in literature, history, and college applications.

UN-DISMISSIVENESS

The Villain is dismissive. In Harry Potter, Voldemort dismisses the magic that he considers beneath him. He views house elves and love as beneath his contempt. The obvious result is that he's defeated by house elves and love. On the other hand, Harry is un-dismissive, creating allies with those dismissed by Voldemort.

Mighty empires often dismiss smaller upstarts before they get defeated by the very underdogs they deride. Churchill referred to Gandhi as a "fakir…striding half-naked." Then, that half-naked fakir and his unarmed followers kicked the British Empire out of India. King George III, referring to the American upstarts, said, "We are determined to listen to nothing from the illegal congress," utterly dismissing the very people who later defeated his massive military.

When describing the United States (who later helped defeat him), Hitler said, "I don't see much future for the Americans … it's a decayed country." When Goliath faced David, he dismissed David before getting defeated by him:

> "When the Philistine [Goliath] looked and saw David, he was contemptuous of him; for he was only a youth, and reddish, with a handsome appearance. So the Philistine said to David, 'Am I a dog, that you come to me with sticks?'"

The dismissiveness of the Villain isn't limited to epic events. That dismissiveness can also be seen in childhood experiences.

A parent who loses his patience in a disagreement might say to a child, "Fine, do whatever you want." Superficially, that statement seems to be what every child wants: total freedom to do anything. But because the statement embodies pure dismissiveness, it is one of the more upsetting things a parent can say to a child.

Legendary comedian George Carlin said, "My job is to point out the things you already knew were funny—you just forgot to laugh at them." In other words, his job is to point out the things that most people dismiss or ignore. His job is to be extremely un-dismissive. Jerry Seinfeld and other masters of observational comedy follow the same principle: they point out the humor in things that most people dismiss.

Christianity became powerful by reaching out to the exact people that society had dismissed. In the Bible, Jesus is notorious for reaching out to those most dismissed by society (the poor, social outcasts, and those with serious diseases). Most other religions do the same. If you're religious, you may believe that connecting with the dismissed is morally right. If you're an atheist, you might at least recognize that doing so is socially powerful.

Villains are dismissive. Heroes aren't. To embody that in your application, you need to be as un-dismissive as possible.

Consider the following two topics: the shapes of dog ears and cancer research. Cancer research is big and important. Everyone cares about it. No one cares about the shapes of dog ears. That makes dog ear shapes the better essay topic. The topic itself is extremely un-dismissive.

Many college essay strategists will tell you to come across as "quirky" in your application. They're 100% right. "Quirky" is just another way of saying "extremely un-dismissive." Quirky people are fascinated by things that other people dismiss.

Let's do a few examples. One common application question asks if you could travel anywhere, where would you go?

The common answers to this are grandiose. The Pyramids, Monaco, the Eiffel Tower, some other Tower, some other gigantic and famous thing. So, let's take one of these and make it interesting by focusing on small things—the very things the Villain would dismiss, but the Hero would care about.

Let's start with the Pyramids. One of the explorers who excavated Egyptian monuments was Giovanni Battista Caviglia. We might be tempted to say we'd like to visit his mansion and view the priceless artifacts he had there. But that's just a different grandiosity. Instead, we can talk about wanting to visit his childhood home, to see the environment that created that curiosity. Or maybe talk about sailing with him on his first merchant ship, getting to talk to him before he was defined by his archaeological discoveries. By the way, discovering these facts required a basic internet search. Expect to do some research for every application question, and a lot of research for most of the questions.

Another option, of course, would be to start with something less famous. Use that thing as a starting point and see what easily dismissed locations you can discover.

Many applications ask students talk about who they would invite to dinner, or who they would invite to give a lecture. Mark Twain, Abraham Lincoln, and Einstein are common answers.

Now, instead of finding easily dismissed details of locations, we need to find easily dismissed people in their lives. For example, you might invite Mark Twain's first grade teacher or Einstein's next-door neighbor to get a different perspective on these giants. Another option would be to pick someone much less famous.

To find people and places that aren't famous, you can't go with common knowledge. Any person you've heard of, everyone has heard of. Instead, use randomization, Wikipedia, and Google to help you find someone less Charted.

For example, you might pick a country, then search poets from that country, then find one you've never heard of, and then find places, people, or things associated with that person.

INVITATION TO THE IVIES

You might pick a year at random, and look at scientific discoveries, books published, or artwork from that year. Use them as starting points for your search and keep exploring until you find something compellingly un-dismissive.

The Hero pays attention to the people and things that the Villain dismisses. Focusing on what others dismiss can help you stand out and get in.

Let's look at a famous college essay that masterfully uses un-dismissiveness. The full text of this essay can be found in the book *Essays that Worked for College Applications* by Curry, Kasbar, and Baer.

The author of the essay, Daniel Burrows, described himself as a person who is easily overlooked but nevertheless important.

> "You see, when all is said and done and everyone has gone home to sleep, I stand there alone; noble and unnoticed. I observe it all. I am the hero's best friend."

Notice that he doesn't cast himself as the Hero, the one who gets all the attention. He makes himself the Hero's best friend, the person most likely to be dismissed. Paradoxically, this extreme un-dismissiveness showcases the best qualities of the Hero archetype.

The author hammers this un-dismissiveness home.

> "It seems that it has always been my part in life to be the second man on the moon or the guy who blocked for the star running back.
>
> "In a world of 'stars,' 'co-stars' and 'special guest stars,' I'm a 'with'; but I always remember my lines and play my character to its fullest.
>
> "I'm the person who places the parsley on your $17.50 Veal Oscar. I never use too much or too little and my little piece of parsley adds style, grace and beauty to your dining experience. Without

my parsley you would detect a vital missing ingredient but would be hard pressed to figure out exactly what it is."

The author shows that he does "small things with great love," to quote Mother Theresa. He's the extreme opposite of dismissive. While his competition jammed their essays with grandiosity, he used un-dismissiveness. He stood out and got in.

Un-dismissiveness will help you shape each of your Four Pillars, including and especially the Intellectual Mission Statement. Picking something un-dismissive as your Activity for Fun or Intellectual Pursuit for Fun is obvious.

But many people fall into the trap of picking something grandiose and obvious for the Intellectual Mission Statement. Resist that temptation! Your Intellectual Mission Statement should focus on something that others dismiss, allowing you to showcase the un-dismissiveness of the Hero and Adult Hero.

DISMISSIVE ESSAYS AND EXTRACURRICULARS THAT DON'T WORK

Villains are dismissive; Heroes are un-dismissive. Villains think big. Voldemort was obsessed with powerful and legendary types of magic like the Elder Wand. The Bond Villain Auric Goldfinger wanted all the gold in Fort Knox. The Borg from *Star Trek* try to assimilate entire planets and races. Lex Luthor wanted to rule Earth as a stepping stone to ruling the entire universe.

Heroes think small. Harry Potter befriended a house elf. Captain Janeway in *Star Trek: Voyager* worked to liberate a single person from the Borg (Seven of Nine).

Extracurriculars and essays that work think small and focus on one thing. The essays and extracurriculars that backfire, on the other hand, tend to think big and lose focus on multiple things.

One of the biggest and most common mistakes that students make is to use lists of information. For example, many students write personal essays that attempt to list many different aspects of their personalities. Usually, these essays use an object, room, TV show, book, or something else as an excuse to list personality attributes.

For example, the essay might be about a cupboard. Each item in the cupboard reminds the student about an favorite activity or personality attribute. A teacup from another country might remind the student that he does Model U.N.; a plate might remind the student that he plays soccer; a bowl might remind the student that he is creative. Thus, while the essay is about one thing (the cupboard), it just turns into a list of attributes.

As another example, an essay might be about a book. The characters in the book remind the student about her own activities and attributes. One character might represent the student's work ethic; another character might represent her love of mathematics. The list continues until the student has listed her resume, bored the reader, and gotten rejected.

We strongly advise against ever writing that type of essay. Lists of information deemphasize each piece of information. In other words, lists are dismissive. List don't show the un-dismissiveness of the Hero or the curiosity or passion that colleges are searching for. Instead, they just show dismissiveness.

For that same reason, we advise against including a lengthy activities resume with your application. An application that has your Four strong Pillars shows passion. An application that has your Four unique Pillars diluted with 20-30 common extracurriculars looks dismissive.

When Arvin was applying to colleges, he included a whopping four page resume that listed activities and awards. He made sure to put everything on there. Of course, it backfired. He ended up getting rejected from almost every college he applied to…including some of his safety schools. He was lucky enough to get into his second-choice school, at least partially because he wasn't able to submit his dismissive, four-page resume to that college.

The long resume conveyed something to the effect of, "Here's a bunch of stuff I did to get in." At the time, that was pretty much exactly his thought process. He had, in fact, done a bunch of stuff just to get in, and the application clearly revealed that attitude. The long list didn't show passion; it showed dismissiveness.

Some students, trying to create Uncharted extracurriculars, end up accidentally creating a list. Many students create resource lists, online portals, databases, etc. on broad topics. For example, a student might create an online portal that contains resources for underprivileged kids to learn about science. Because it's just a list of information on a common topic, it fails strategically. The topic is common, and the presentation is dismissive. It's the worst of both worlds.

Lists are inherently dismissive. Whether that list is a list of resources to help kids learn about math, an essay that finds an excuse to list your character traits and extracurriculars, or a multi-page extracurricular resume, the list will backfire, show dismissiveness, and almost always lead to rejection letters.

Depth shows passion. Breadth shows dismissiveness. Depth beats breadth every time.

THE EXCEPTION

Earlier chapters discuss rarity and completeness. If something is not rare, but has been done to an exceptional level, it can work. For example, if you play tennis (an extremely common extracurricular) and then win Wimbledon (taking the extracurricular to an exceptional level), it will definitely help you get into an Ivy.

Something similar applies to lists. If you make a list, it becomes world famous, and it showcases one or more of the Three Archetypes, it could work.

As examples, Craigslist and Angie's List are both lists. However, both were groundbreaking (showcasing the Hero), and both are world famous, household names. Their success level is also easily quantifiable, which can help show exceptional completeness. Craigslist makes hundreds of millions of dollars a year. Angie's List makes over a billion dollars a year. Both companies have reached an exceptional level of completeness, even if their concepts aren't particularly unusual.

If you were the founder of Craigslist or Angie's List, that would certainly help you get into an Ivy.

Goop, the lifestyle brand created by actress Gwyneth Paltrow, is also essentially a list of products, combined with a few Goop-branded products. It's also a household name that earns tens of millions in revenue per year. Goop incorporates both the Adult Hero and the Nerd (which we'll talk about in the next chapter). The fact that Paltrow overcame heavy initial opposition showcases the perseverance of the Hero and the Guide-rejection of the Adult Hero.

If you founded Goop, that would help you get into an Ivy.

But while world famous, groundbreaking lists can help, the remaining 99.99% of lists hurt.

Instead of trying to include everything, think small. Focus on one or two Uncharted interests and make them the Pillars of your application.

THE NERD

So far, we have the Hero vs the Victim and the Adult Hero vs the Villain. Let's look at the final archetype pair: the Nerd vs the Sociopath.

The Nerd is driven by curiosity about small things. The Sociopath is driven by status about big things.

To imagine the Sociopath, don't think about a serial killer (psychopath); instead think about the worst stereotypes about investment bankers, driven entirely by greed and status.

Nerds like to learn. Sociopaths like to win. Ivies try to let in Nerds and keep out Sociopaths. Sounds easy, right?

Not quite. Sociopaths and Nerds often look nearly the same on paper.

Nerds get high SAT scores and grades because they are curious about math and reading. Sociopaths get high SAT scores and grades because they want to win the Ivy admissions competition. Thus, looking at SAT scores can't help colleges differentiate between the Nerd and the Sociopath.

What about community service? Nerds do it because they believe in the cause. Sociopaths do it to boost their college resumes.

Fortunately, there are two key differences between the Nerd and Sociopath archetypes that Ivies can detect. Embodying them in your application will help you come across as the Nerd archetype and get in.

You already know one of them: un-dismissiveness. Nerds are incredibly un-dismissive. While everyone around them is pursuing wealth and status, Nerds are fascinated by the other, commonly overlooked topics. That's one more reason to make sure your Four Pillars focus on small, commonly overlooked topics. The more un-dismissive your Pillars are, the more you are likely to portray the Nerd rather than the Sociopath.

The other difference is curiosity. Nerds are intensely curious. Sociopaths, like narcissists, believe that they already know everything.

INVITATION TO THE IVIES

If you know everything, there's not much to be curious about. Thus, showcasing curiosity will help you portray the Nerd archetype.

Let's start with the obvious way to showcase curiosity: ask questions. Specifically, ask your high school teachers questions.

If you ask your teachers questions, that will usually convince them that you are curious. They will then describe your curiosity in your recommendation letters, which will help you stand out and get in.

Let's look at a few hypothetical examples to illustrate how curiosity can improve your teacher recommendations. Consider this teacher recommendation:

> Fred is the smartest student in the entire school. He works hard, gets the highest grades on exams, and gets the highest grades on homework assignments.

At first, that seems like a top-notch recommendation. But there's a huge problem. There are 35,000 high schools in the country. At each high school, someone gets the highest grades. Thus, there are 35,000 students with the highest grades in their respective schools.

Harvard only lets in 2,000 or fewer students a year. So as positive as the above recommendation is, it doesn't come close to describing a rare applicant. Although this recommendation appears to be excellent, it has virtually no chance of working.

Let's take a look at another recommendation.

> Fred asks the most interesting questions during class. I find myself thinking about the questions after class, discussing them with my colleagues, and even using them to guide discussions of later classes.

This recommendation describes something far more rare. There isn't one student in every high school who asks compelling and interesting questions. There isn't one student in every 10 high schools, or one in 100 high schools, who asks compelling questions.

More importantly, this recommendation clearly shows the Nerd, not the Sociopath. The Nerd is defined by curiosity. The Sociopath is defined by ambition and self-interest. The Nerd is extremely rare among competitive students; competitive students are usually driven by ambition more than curiosity.

Asking questions is more important than getting high grades. Almost every Ivy applicant has high grades. Very few ever ask any questions at all, let alone any good ones.

But not all questions work. Only the questions that appear to be motivated by genuine curiosity work. Let's look at a few common errors.

Questions about grades don't work. Grades are the domain of the Sociopath. The Sociopath is motivated by prestige and success and thus works to get the highest grades possible. A question like, "Will this be on the test?" is a Sociopath question, not a Nerd question. Similarly, "What percentage of our grade will come from homework?" is a Sociopath question.

Here are a few more common Sociopath questions to avoid:

- "Will there be extra credit?"
- "Will this be on the exam?"
- "Is an 89.5 an A?"
- "What can I do to improve my grade?"

Any question about grades is purely in the domain of the Sociopath.

Questions about how to solve a problem aren't Nerd questions either. They aren't as damaging as questions about grades, but they aren't helpful either. "How do you do this question?" isn't a real Nerd question. "I'm stuck," also isn't a Nerd question. Neither is "Can you show me how to do this?"

In fact, those questions convey the Victim. Remember, the Victim's job is to ask for help. That doesn't mean asking for help is wrong. If you need help understanding a subject, ask for it.

But those questions don't count as Nerd questions. They don't have strategic value.

Nerd questions are questions about the subject itself or its application. Here are a few examples:

- "What is the flame of a fire made out of?"
- "Why can't you go below absolute zero?"
- "How is it possible to have negative decibels?"
- "If a brass instrument were made of steel, would it sound the same?"
- "Why do tarantulas have hair, if they're cold blooded?"

Notice that none of the Nerd questions has any value for grades, social status, getting into Honors classes, getting awards, making money, etc. The only reason to ask these types of questions is curiosity.

Many parents complain of a distinct lack of curiosity in their kids. This is a completely learned behavior. There is no human being on the planet that is genuinely not curious at all. This is perfectly evident when you look at any baby in any country, culture, or time period. It is basic human nature to be intensely curious.

All infants are curious. So are all young children. High school (and to a lesser extent middle school) seems to destroy that curiosity.

But that curiosity isn't gone. It's still right there. Why do "clickbait" articles work? When people click on them, are they expecting to get higher grades or make more money? Of course not. When you watch a random YouTube video that catches your eye, are you expecting higher grades? Nope.

Your curiosity isn't gone. You've just been in an environment that removes the joy and curiosity from learning.

Hard as it is to believe, that's good news. Your competition is stuck in that same environment. Their curiosity is also buried. They won't be asking Nerd questions any time soon.

They don't know what you know. They don't know how important those Nerd questions are for Ivy strategy. You'll be able to ask the most Nerd questions because most of your competitors won't be asking any.

We recommend asking at least one question per two weeks in each class. Don't tell your teacher you're doing that, obviously. And don't give it away by asking the question on the same day and time every week. Mix it up. Ask some during class. Ask some during office hours or extra help.

If you're shy, that's okay. You can ask the questions after class, during office hours, or by sending an email. If asking questions in front of the entire class is intimidating, find a way to ask your teacher directly.

To ask the best questions, you should get ahead in the class. Always study the information two chapters ahead. This gives you an advanced perspective on the subject that helps you ask better questions. You can also put your full focus into creating those questions. While everyone else is learning the material for the first time, you will already know it, and can thus focus entirely on asking questions.

Ideally, you should complete the course material before the school year starts. For example, you can learn calculus in the summer before calculus is taught at your school.

Obviously, don't let your teacher know you did that! Advanced learning is a secret weapon that will help you seem naturally adept with the material and give you the mental space to focus on creating great questions.

Never ask questions about grades, no matter what. Don't worry; there's still a way to get the information. If you want to know if a particular chapter will be on the exam, you don't need to ask. Just wait. Someone else will ask for you. That person will hurt his Ivy chances; you won't have to hurt your own.

What if a test gets misgraded? That also has an easy solution. Just ask the teacher to help you understand the answer. The teacher will see the error and fix your grade automatically. You won't have to ask for a regrade.

If your parents are involved with your education, show them this chapter. Your parents must be on board with this part. You should never ask about grades, and neither should they. Often, parents try to help students by asking teachers about grades. To make things worse, they sometimes say things like, "My son/daughter is really worried about his grade." A sentence like that can heavily damage your Ivy strategy.

Instead, make sure your parents are part of your strategy. They need to say things like, "He doesn't care about grades," and "He loves the subject." Your parents should emphasize your curiosity, and never mention grades at all (other than to point out that you don't care about them).

All this will help your teacher confirm that you're motivated by real curiosity. The trait of curiosity is so incredibly rare that a teacher recommendation that mentions it will give your application a huge boost.

The other way to show curiosity is through your Four Pillars. Your Pillars should involve Exploration of the Uncharted in a way that has nothing to do with making money. The Intellectual Pursuit for Fun is the obvious area to showcase this, but you should bring the Nerd into all four of the Pillars. Let's look at how that works.

NERD KNOWLEDGE

Nerds embody curiosity and un-dismissiveness. They ask questions and explore areas that others don't.

One result of this is that Nerds know things that other people don't. Showing this type of knowledge will help you make colleges perceive you as the Nerd.

Nerd knowledge isn't more knowledge on common subjects. Nerds don't know more AP physics than Sociopaths. They don't know more about Picasso than Sociopaths. Instead, they know facts about people and topics that are off the beaten path.

Those who are driven by their inner Nerds find these facts as they go through their normal life. If your inner Nerd is running the show, you probably already know facts about subjects that most people haven't thought about. You might know about sculptors that others don't know about. You might have opinions on ancient religions that other people haven't ever heard of.

But most teenagers in competitive environments aren't really led by their inner Nerds. Let's talk about how to access Nerd knowledge, even if your inner Nerd is dormant.

Suppose you start with Art. The goal is to find facts about art that no one else knows. You do a Google search to find strange facts about art.

When we do this exercise in our Ivy Strategy seminars, something funny happens. Almost every student comes up with the same facts.

The common saying is, "Great minds think alike." The historically accurate saying is, "Great minds think alike, but fools seldom differ." Many students, when doing what they are certain is clever and original, end up doing the exact same thing as thousands of their competitors.

Competitive students do the same extracurriculars as other competitive students. They do the same Model U.N., Chemistry Olympiads, Business Decas, Debate Clubs, violin lessons, nursing home volunteering, etc.

Competitive students sometimes come to the realization that all their competitors are adding the exact same activities to their resumes. Unfortunately, competitive students then often come up with…more of the same activities as "solutions" to this problem, usually thinking that they are the first to come up with such an idea.

For example, many students play instruments and volunteer at nursing homes or VA hospitals. Then, they all have the same idea: they will play their instruments at those nursing homes or VA hospitals. This is not new or unique; it's not on the level of an Ivy application at all.

Similarly, when coming up with Nerd knowledge, most competitive students come up with the exact same knowledge. They look up interesting facts about art, architecture, philosophy, history, chemistry, music, or literature, and they come up with the same facts that our students before them also came up with.

Fortunately, there's a way to overcome that and find facts about a subject that your competition won't also discover. It involves using a Randomization Element.

For this example, the goal is to find facts about art that your competition won't also know. To start, go ahead and pick a random year. For this example, we can pick the year 1950.

Then, search for 1950 in art and find the Wikipedia page for 1950 in art.

On that page, there are some artists mentioned that are extremely famous; for example, Dali, Chagall, Matisse, and Pollock. Avoid those ones.

But then, there are artists that are not at all famous. They're famous enough to make it to the Wikipedia page, but not famous enough to be household names. We can call them the "Unfamous" artists.

The Unfamous artists are the ones you want. Those are the artists that the Nerd would know about, but the Sociopath wouldn't. When looking at this page, the Sociopath would be drawn to the most famous artists. He believes that there could be a situation in life in which a bit more knowledge about Dali could benefit him. But the Nerd is drawn to the Unfamous artists, the ones that are important but obscure.

Let's go ahead and pick one of those artists. The goal is to find interesting facts. With the Randomization Element (a randomly chosen year), there is virtually no chance that a competing student will pick the same artist. For this example, we'll pick Albert Giacometti. We chose him because we hadn't heard of him.

The next step is to go to Giacometti's Wikipedia page and find interesting facts about him. But be careful. The facts must be interesting and NOT in the domain of the Sociopath. That means that the facts should not be about money, fame, status, prestige, or power.

The page says that he was born in Borgonovo, Switzerland. Isn't that interesting?

Of course not. That's entirely uninteresting. Can you imagine how you'd feel if someone said to you, "Oh I heard the coolest thing. Alberto Giacometti was born in Borgonovo, Switzerland!"

His year of birth is also uninteresting. His parents' names are uninteresting. The fact that he is the oldest child is uninteresting. The fact that he moved to Paris is uninteresting.

The fact that his solo exhibition at the National Portrait Gallery got five-star reviews is also uninteresting…and shows the Sociopath. Good reviews, fame, and fortune are the domain of the Sociopath, not the Nerd.

INVITATION TO THE IVIES

So, let's find Nerd facts. You may notice that the Nerd facts "feel" right. In other words, the facts by themselves have the "X-factors" that you'll find in a successful college essay...or a cool movie, story, or poem.

For 6 years, his sculptures had a maximum height of 2.75 inches. He said, "But wanting to create from memory what I had seen, to my terror the sculpture became smaller and smaller."

That fact, by itself, could be a cool opening for an Ivy essay. You could use it to develop an Intellectual Pursuit for Fun or an Activity for Fun.

It also is something worth telling. A sculptor tried to create realism from memory, but the more he tried to do that, the smaller the sculptures became. That's something it could be interesting to talk about. Can size betray realism?

Using this as a starting point, you could develop an Intellectual Mission Statement around the sizes of ancient monoliths or tiny ancient figurines, and the associated impact on the cultures of the era.

At the very least, it would be more interesting to talk about than the year he was born.

Later, when his sculptures started getting taller, we find out that "the larger they grew, the thinner they became." That's another interesting nuance.

With Randomization Elements, finding Nerd knowledge can be easy and fun. If you do this exercise a few times, you may discover things about artists, musicians, mathematicians, and philosophers that genuinely intrigue you.

Randomization Elements can help you unlock Nerd knowledge. The most common Randomization Elements are years. For example, choosing artists, architects, poets, musicians, etc. from a randomly chosen year, you'll find people and ideas that essentially no other competitive student will know about.

Randomization Elements don't have to be years. They can be counties or towns. For example, looking only at one randomly chosen county or city can unlock obscure but interesting artists, writers, philosophers, and the like.

Some worry that choosing to talk about an "Unfamous" artist rather than a household name artist will seem unbelievable to Ivies. How could someone stumble across an Unfamous artist at all? You might wonder how anyone could learn about any artist that isn't taught in art history class at school.

The fact is, most students don't know about Unfamous artists, or Unfamous philosophers, or Unfamous anything. They only know about the most famous people. Also, most students get rejected. 95% of highly competitive students get rejected from Harvard. Harvard is looking for something that 19 out of 20 elite students don't have.

Unfamous people aren't as obscure as they seem, by the way. Alberto Giacometti is on Swiss currency.

Knowing about Unfamous artists or philosophers is common among Nerds. All Nerds know about Unfamous artists, philosophers, scientists, etc. The endless curiosity of the Nerd ensures it.

On the other hand, the Sociopath almost never knows about Unfamous people. Thus, merely having knowledge about Unfamous people shows that you embody the Nerd, rather than the Sociopath.

THE POWER OF THE NERD

The Nerd showcases more power than the Sociopath.

You read that right. For all the Sociopath's relentlessness and ambition, the Nerd looks more powerful.

Most people spend the vast majority of their time and energy focusing on survival. They may strive to get a financially lucrative job so they can have the money for survival. They may strive for higher social status as a means of ensuring survival. Most of us, driven by fear and ego, focus on survival and the things that support survival: money, prestige, and power.

When we seek knowledge, most of us want to use that knowledge to get more money, prestige, or power.

The Nerd, on the other hand, is driven by curiosity for its own sake. At a primal level, this showcases true power. The Nerd appears so certain of his survival that he doesn't need to worry about money, prestige, or power. To the rest of us who are clawing our way to the top, this is staggeringly strange.

Showcasing the Nerd is showcasing strength and fearlessness. When you show knowledge of topics that have nothing to do with power or prestige, it seems that you have more than enough power and prestige and are free to pursue other interests. Since almost no one else feels like that, it makes you look superhuman.

That's why it's critical to make sure your Nerd knowledge has nothing to do with power or prestige. Information about the fastest car, the tallest building, the most expensive hotel, etc., just shows an obsession with power and prestige. It makes you look like everyone else. On the other hand, if you know about things that have nothing to do with power or prestige, you stand above the fray among the elite.

For your Four Pillars, you should obviously have Nerd knowledge for the Intellectual Pursuit for Fun and the Intellectual Mission Statement.

But you should also discover Nerd knowledge for the Activity for Fun and the Activity for Service. For example, suppose your Activity for Service involves creating a new type of safety seal for household cleaners. You should make sure to learn Nerd facts about safety seals, their history, and their invention to showcase the Nerd.

INVITATION TO THE IVIES

BUSINESS SCHOOL

This section is only for those applying to an undergraduate business school, such as Wharton.

If you're applying to an undergraduate business school, the most important thing to do is to emphasize the Nerd and avoid the tiniest hint of the Sociopath archetype. Along with the Nerd, you should also use the Hero and Adult Hero archetypes.

Here are a few rules:

1. Never talk about wanting to make money.
2. Never talk about wanting financial success.
3. Never talk about financial security.
4. Just avoid money entirely.

This might seem like bizarre advice. After all, isn't the whole point of business to make money? Isn't everyone applying to business school specifically hoping to make money?

Probably. But first, if everyone is doing something, then it's bad strategy since it won't stand out.

But more than that, top business schools are looking for people who will use business to change the world, not just make money.

John Mackey, founder of Whole Foods, put it well:

> "You can't live if you don't eat, but you don't live to eat. And neither does business exist primarily to make a profit. It exists to fulfill its purpose, whatever that might be."

A business needs money, but the goal of a business should be something other than making money. John Mackey's book *Conscious Capitalism* explores this idea deeply.

The center of a successful undergraduate business school application is an Uncharted goal that will benefit the world. Many companies, including tech companies, medical companies, infrastructure companies, tool companies, and transportation companies have benefited the world. To do that, they also needed to be profitable. But their contributions were not their personal profits, but rather advances in tech, medicine, etc.

To get into a competitive undergraduate business school, you should develop an Uncharted Pillar that could turn into a business, is already a business, or could guide an existing business. This will usually be your Activity for Service, but in some cases can be the Activity for Fun.

The business can be a nonprofit, by the way. Nonprofits need to make enough money to survive if they want to pursue their goals. As always, the rarer and more complete it is, the better.

With Wharton in particular, completeness beats everything else. Many applicants have a cool business idea. Very few have done anything at all with it. Taking an idea farther than your competition will help you stand out and get in.

Many students make the same mistake: they accidentally embody the Sociopath in their application. For example, they join clubs that focus purely on the profit side of business, rather than the helping humanity aspect of business. The most common example is building an application around clubs and extracurriculars that focus on investing.

Such clubs can hurt your application, as they broadcast the Sociopath archetype. Investing for the sake of making money only removes the building and creating parts of business, and amps up the profit-making part of business. If you're trading stocks, your goal isn't to create anything at all; it's just to make money. It might be a great thing to do in real life, but it's a terrible thing to build an application around.

Let's look at what Wharton itself says about its undergraduate program. The website opens with a simple tag line: "Explore ideas, think strategically, make an impact." Note that "make money" and "make profit" aren't on there.

The site then continues to focus on the impact part of business rather than the profit part:

> "Business makes things happen and affects every part of society. At Wharton, the world's premier business school, you will gain knowledge and experience you need to become a leader in business and make a positive impact on today's challenging economic and social issues."

Again, it's about how you positively affect the world, not about how much money you make.

To drive the point home, Wharton includes a few student profiles. None of them are about making money. Many are about social impact, and others are about personal discovery and development.

Instead of focusing on investing or cryptocurrency trading, focus on the parts of business that create something Uncharted. Entrepreneurship is the obvious example. Building a small business around an Uncharted idea that has a positive impact can improve your application.

Starting a nonprofit is another great option. The key to a nonprofit is you have to do it yourself. You can't have your parents do it. That especially includes the boring initial parts that involve filling out forms, submitting them, resubmitting them, etc.

Parental nonprofits (nonprofits entirely organized by parents but done in the student's name) are incredibly easy to tell apart from nonprofits organized by students. When detected, they can damage an application's chances of success.

Parental nonprofits also cause problems when students answer essay and interview questions. For example, when a student answers an essay or interview question about the first challenge they faced when starting a nonprofit, and the nonprofit is genuine, the answers usually involve difficulty with paperwork, not being taken seriously by family and friends, internal self-doubt, unwillingness of adults to take teenagers seriously, struggling to get meetings with the people they needed to, etc.

On the other hand, when it's a parental nonprofit, students often say things like, "The first challenge I faced with my nonprofit was curing homelessness." Answers like that immediately let the interviewer or essay reader know that the student had no real involvement with the nonprofit.

Some students ask if putting a twist on investing can work. For example, green investing, ethical investing, and the like appear to be different from regular investing. In one important way, they are: they don't embody the Sociopath archetype.

But they usually run into another problem: lack of rarity. Green investing already exists. Ethical investing, politically focused investing, investing in women-owned businesses, etc. already exist. If you come up with a genuinely new and clever twist on investing, that can work. But the common ones generally fail due to lack of rarity and lack of Unchartedness.

If something has already been done, or something similar has already been done, you would need to take it to a staggering level of completeness to make it work. For example, if you started a multibillion-dollar hedge fund with an ethical component while still in high school, that would work. Obviously, it would have to be a fund you started, not something your parents started and put your name on.

On the other hand, if you start a green investing club at school, it probably won't stand out enough to matter. There are just too many similar clubs in the country, and many of their founders are also applying to Wharton.

If you're applying to an undergraduate business school, don't make your Four Pillars about money; instead make them about building and creating new and Uncharted things that serve a specific need and improve a specific part of the human experience.

INTERVIEWS AND THE ARCHETYPES

We've talked about how to make your Ivy admissions interviews focus on your Four Pillars. However, that might not work for some questions. For other questions, you can rely on the Hero, Adult Hero, and Nerd archetypes. You can use these archetypes to enhance your interview answers about your Four Pillars.

The Nerd

The Nerd is defined by curiosity. The first way to showcase the Nerd is to ask questions.

In any college interview or job interview, the questions you ask matter more than the answers you give. Good questions beat good answers.

At the end of most college interviews, the interviewer will ask if you have any questions. The worst possible thing you can say is, "No, not really." (By the way, that is the most common answer.)

Instead, you should ask questions that meet the following criteria:

1. They cannot be answered with a Google search. For example, "How many majors does Yale offer?" is a terrible question. Just look it up.
2. They can't be so specific that no interviewer would know the answer. For example, "What type of questions are on the exam for Differential Equations Part 2?" is a terrible question.
3. They should not be logistical. For example, "Would my credits from a semester in France and one in Spain transfer directly?" is a terrible question.
4. They should avoid the Sociopath. For example, "What should I do to get in?" is a terrible question. It showcases the Sociopath instead of the Nerd.
5. They should involve the interviewer's personal experience. For example, "Were there any professors who changed your mind about

something?" is a great question. "What surprised you about the college?" is also a great question. "What would you change about the college?" is great as well. (Warning: Almost every interviewer answers that they wish the college better addressed financial inequality. Have a follow-up question or comment ready.)

You'll get a chance to ask questions at the end….but you don't need to wait until the end to ask a question. Instead, try to ask questions throughout the interview.

If you can't ask questions earlier, then feel free to ask more than one question at the end. Don't make it weird; ask 2-3 questions, not 200.

The Nerd is all about curiosity. Asking good questions showcases the Nerd.

The Hero

The Hero proves himself through persistence…but that's not how we recognize the Hero. We recognize the Hero the moment she steps into Uncharted Territory.

To show the Hero, make your questions and answers all about Uncharted Territory. Let's look at a few examples.

Question: What are you most excited about at College X?

Non-Hero Answer: I'm most excited to learn new things from amazing professors. (If you're learning something that someone else knows, you're in Charted Territory.)

Hero Answer: I'm excited to do research on [your Intellectual Mission Statement].

Also Hero Answer: I'm excited to do an entrepreneurship in [Your Intellectual Mission Statement, Activity for Service, or Activity for Fun].

Hero answers focus on Uncharted Territory, not on Charted Territory.

Question: Why do you want to major in _____?

Non-Hero Answer: I want to learn more about _____ so I can get a job using my knowledge.

That is Charted Territory, not Uncharted Territory.

Hero Answer: I want to major in _____ because I want to push the boundaries of [your Intellectual Mission Statement or Intellectual Pursuit for Fun].

Question: Where do you hope to be in 10 years?

Non-Hero Answer: I hope to have comfortable job as a _____.

Hero Answer: I hope to be exploring and collaborating on [your Intellectual Mission Statement or Intellectual Pursuit for Fun].

Question: What would you do if you won the lottery?

Non-Hero Answer: I would buy a fancy house and car.

Also NON-Hero Answer: I would fund research in [your Intellectual Mission Statement].

Why doesn't that one work? It's about research; shouldn't that be enough?

You probably know that Leonardo da Vinci painted the Mona Lisa. You probably know that Michelangelo sculpted the statue of David. But, without looking it up, do you know who commissioned the Mona Lisa or the statue of David? Most people don't.

We don't care about the people who funded the exploration of Uncharted Territory; we care about the people who did the exploration. Most people don't know who funded famous voyages or commissioned great works of art. We know the explorers, not the funders.

Here's the Hero answer: I would create a research lab (or entrepreneurial incubator or research and development program) with the best equipment to research [your Intellectual Mission Statement]. I'd hire the greatest thinkers in the fields of _____, _____, and _____, and we'd all work together to figure out _____.

Heroes don't fund exploration; they DO exploration. They might also fund it; the great astronomer Tycho Brahe funded his own research. However, he's famous for the research, not for being rich. He's famous because he explored Uncharted Territory.

To bring in the Hero archetype, show an interest in exploring Uncharted Territory.

The Adult Hero

The Hero becomes an Adult Hero when he rejects a fundamental view of the Guide. How on earth can you bring that archetype into an interview?

One highly impractical option would be to introduce a Guide in an answer, and then reject the guide in the answer. There might be some cases in which you can make that work. But there's a much easier way to do it: reject the premise of the question.

Rejecting the premise of a question means rejecting an assumption that the question relies on. In this situation, the Guide becomes the guidelines of the question itself. The guidelines are often implied, rather than stated directly. By rejecting those unstated guidelines, you can showcase the Adult Hero.

Let's look at examples of how to answer questions using that technique.

Question: What are you most excited to learn about in college?

Adult Hero Answer: I'm more excited about unlearning than learning. By unlearning, I mean figuring out what assumptions I've made that can go and how moving past them can show something surprising.

Question: If you could be any character in The Lord of the Rings, who would you be?

Adult Hero Answer: I wouldn't choose an official character; I'd want to be the 3rd person narrator, the observer.

Now that you know how the three major archetypes can be used in interviews, let's see how we can use them to improve interview answers.

Question: If you could witness any event in history, what would you choose?

Initial Answer: I'd like to be there when the Wright Brothers finally flew for the first time, disproving their detractors, and showing their greatness.

This answer showcases the Sociopath. The Sociopath is pure Ego, obsessed with status, prestige, adulation of the masses, and being right.

Let's change this a bit to showcase the Hero. We recognize the Hero by the moment she steps into Uncharted Territory.

Improved Answer: I'd like to witness the moment when the Wright brothers decided they were going to try to build a flying machine.

The true Heroic moment isn't the moment of victory; it's the moment that the Hero steps into Uncharted Territory. That's why we celebrate July 4th, the date of the signing of the Declaration of Independence when the colonists stepped into Uncharted Territory rather than September 3rd, the date the colonies formally gained independence.

That's why you should talk about witnessing the moment the Wright brothers made their decision to build a flying machine. The moment of greatness is the very first step into the Uncharted. That is the moment that will showcase you as a Hero, even if you're only talking about witnessing it.

Let's use that principle on another one:

Question: Tell me about a time when you had to be a leader.

Initial answer: I was a leader when my _____ team won the national championship.

Improved Heroic Answer: I was a leader when I encouraged my _____ team to try out a totally new strategy. We ended up winning the national championship.

Before any interview, you should prepare with some basic research. Some people with a lot of interview experience appear to go into interviews with no preparation at all. To an outsider, for example, Arvin may appear to go into interviews without preparation.

But in reality, he prepares for every single interview. His "secret" is that he doesn't try to memorize everything on the topic. Instead, he finds just one fact or quote to bring up during the interview. He then tries to think of something insightful to say about that one fact or quote during the interview.

Here's what Arvin would do if he were a student doing a college interview.

1. Skim the headlines of the college newspaper (e.g., the Harvard Crimson).
2. Watch a few minutes of a YouTube clip of one professor from the college.
3. Come up with something insightful to say about either an article or the professor's clip, most likely inspired by the three archetypes.

Then, during the interview, he would find a way to bring up the clip or article and mention the insight.

Why not watch 20 videos and come up with 20 insights? It would be too much to keep straight in a high-pressure interview. For that matter, it would be too much to keep straight for a casual conversation. Make a list of 20 things in your head right now and see if you can casually fit every single thing into a conversation with a parent or friend. Most people won't get past the third thing.

5

THE THREE RHETORICAL TECHNIQUES

We've discussed the Four Pillars and the Three Archetypes that can help you shape them. Now let's look at a few useful essay writing techniques that can help you present your Four Pillars and showcase the personality archetypes that are the most useful.

There are three Rhetorical Techniques we'll discuss in this book: Reversals, Analogical Reasoning, and Categorization. These incredibly powerful techniques are used not only in Ivy essays, but also in everything from standup comedy to theology.

You will use these techniques on application essays and short answer questions. You should also use these on blog posts you write, books you write, and some of the videos you make as part of developing your Four Pillars. Finally, you can use the Three Rhetorical Techniques to create Pillars.

In addition, you should start using them in your history and English papers in school. This is especially important if you're applying to Princeton. As part of the Princeton application, you will need to submit one graded English paper from school. That paper will be examined for two things. First, it will be examined for the quality of your intellectual thought. Second, it will be compared to your application essays to see if you wrote your own essays, instead of having someone else write them. Start using these techniques in 9th or 10th grade to ensure that the English paper you submit with your application matches the writing style of your application essays.

REVERSALS

The first technique is the Reversal. We already described it a bit when we discussed the Adult Hero archetype. In fact, the Reversal is a rhetorical expression of the Adult Hero archetype. Reversals symbolizes the act of rejecting a fundamental view of the Guide. Reversals allow you to present yourself as the Adult Hero, the most inspiring of all archetypes.

Reversals aren't just Ivy essay techniques. These incredibly powerful archetypal tools are used by famous poets, comedians, politicians, novelists, filmmakers, and artists.

The Guide that a Reversal rejects might be a person, but Reversals can also be disagreements with prevailing or expected viewpoints or disagreements with inspiring quotes. They can also be clever twists and inversions of common sayings or opinions. Let's look at famous examples. You might recognize a few of them from school, TV, or independent reading, but now you'll be able to see why they are so powerful. Rejecting a Guide embodies the Adult Hero and is thus inherently inspiring and magnetic.

We'll start with one of the most famous and intriguing openings in English poetry, the opening of T.S. Eliot's "The Wasteland":

> April is the cruellest month, breeding
> Lilacs out of the dead land, mixing
> Memory and desire, stirring
> Dull roots with spring rain.
>
> Winter kept us warm, covering
> Earth in forgetful snow, feeding
> A little life with dried tubers.

In this opening, there are multiple Reversals. Normally, we see spring as happy because winter ends and flowers grow. Eliot reverses that view, saying that April is the "cruellest" month because it forces us to confront what we've left buried in our minds. We can no longer stay numb, but instead must face reality.

Normally, we see winter as cold. Eliot says that winter kept us warm, because it gave us the comfort of forgetting unpleasant thoughts and memories.

Usually, a poem as dense and difficult to understand as "The Wasteland" would struggle for lasting fame. However, the opening is so simple, so unforgettable, and has such strong Reversals that the opening line and the poem itself continue to be among the most remembered of all poems in the English language.

Reversals aren't limited to difficult poetry. Consider the book *Watchmen*, one of the only graphic novels to make it to TIME Magazine's list of best novels of the 20th century. It has also been turned into a brutal action movie, an HBO series, and a video game.

In its most famous scene, the vigilante Rorschach has been arrested and sent to prison with many of the criminals he sent there. He's locked in a concrete building with his enemies, hugely outnumbered.

The criminals taunt and threaten him continuously. Then, in the cafeteria line, he suddenly stabs one inmate and throws boiling oil on another. As the guards drag him away, he famously calls out, "None of you seem to understand. I'm not locked in here with you. You're locked in here with ME!"

He takes the common view (it's bad to be locked in a prison with dozens of people who want to kill you for revenge) and reverses it (those dozens of people are the ones in danger). His words evoke the Adult Hero and the inspiration that goes along with it.

Reversals don't have to be sad, angry, or violent. Eastern philosopher and cult leader Osho Rajneesh takes a common quote and reverses it in a way that is uplifting and inspiring:

> "People say love is blind because they do not know what love is. I say unto you, only love has eyes; other than love, everything is blind."

Listeners don't just find the quote inspiring; they find Osho himself inspiring. The quote inspires the audience and clearly puts Osho in the role of Adult Hero.

Clever comedians can put multiple Reversals together. Here's one from comedian Dmitri Martin. He takes a common view and reverses it, twists it, and creates something both unforgettable and firmly in the realm of the Adult Hero. Here's what he says:

> "Those who see the glass half full are considered optimists. Yeah. But shouldn't we be more specific about the contents of the glass? If it is a glass of shit then I'm going half empty. I don't like shit. As an optimist, yeah, A half empty shit glass right here, so don't worry about it."

The text by itself is memorable; the video is better. This comedy routine contains reversals that cast Martin as the Adult Hero. He rejects the Guide (in this case, the common view).

Now let's see how G.K. Chesterton, world famous theologian, reverses a similar view. He's going to talk about the optimist and pessimist in a more elevated way than Martin. However, he still rejects the guide and establishes himself as the Adult Hero, the most magnetic of all archetypes.

> "When I was a boy there were two curious men running about who were called the optimist and the pessimist. I constantly used

> the words myself, but I cheerfully confess that I never had any very special idea of what they meant. The only thing which might be considered evident was that they could not mean what they said; for the ordinary verbal explanation was that the optimist thought this world as good as it could be, while the pessimist thought it as bad as it could be. Both these statements being obviously raving nonsense, one had to cast about for other explanations. An optimist could not mean a man who thought everything right and nothing wrong. For that is meaningless; it is like calling everything right and nothing left. Upon the whole, I came to the conclusion that the optimist thought everything good except the pessimist, and that the pessimist thought everything bad, except himself."

Other parts of theology also showcase the Adult Hero. Jesus is also an archetypal Adult Hero. He repeatedly rejected the prevailing views of his time. He rejected both the religious and political establishments. Moses, too, is an archetypal Adult Hero.

Sometimes, a reversal can be entirely contained in a simple quote. Let's look at a quote from world famous short story writer, Jessamyn West:

> "Fiction reveals truth that reality obscures."

In a single sentence, West intrigues the reader and clearly establishes herself as an Adult Hero.

Here's legendary comedian Jerry Seinfeld using a few clever reversals, and embodying the Adult Hero:

> "So, I move into the center lane, now I get ahead of this woman, who felt for some reason I guess, that she thought that I cut her off. So, she pulls up alongside of me, gives me the finger. It seems like such an arbitrary, ridiculous thing to just pick a finger and you

show it to the person. It's a finger, what does it mean? Someone shows me one of their fingers and I'm supposed to feel bad. Is that the way it's supposed to work? I mean, you could just give someone the toe, really, couldn't you? I would feel worse if I got the toe than if I got the finger. 'Cause it's not easy to give someone the toe, you've gotta get the shoe off, the sock off and drive, get it up and… (Jerry pretends to drive with one foot in the air, giving the toe.) 'Look at that toe, buddy.' (He puts his foot down.) I mean, that's really insulting to get the toe, isn't it?"

The standard view (The Guide) is that giving the finger is insulting. Seinfeld's view is that giving the toe is insulting. He rejects the Guide and comes across as the Adult Hero (and also funny).

And here's a great one from Oscar Wilde's A Picture of Dorian Gray:

"The only artists I have ever known who are personally delightful are bad artists. Good artists exist simply in what they make, and consequently are perfectly uninteresting in what they are. A great poet, a really great poet, is the most unpoetical of all creatures. But inferior poets are absolutely fascinating. The worse their rhymes are, the more picturesque they look. The mere fact of having published a book of second-rate sonnets makes a man quite irresistible. He lives the poetry that he cannot write. The others write the poetry that they dare not realize."

The standard view is that great poets are interesting people. The reversed view is that bad poets are interesting people.

Soccer superstar Cristiano Ronaldo is also known for his Reversals. Here's a classic one:

"Dreams are not what you see in your sleep, they are the things that don't let you sleep."

Among leaders, visionaries, and inspirers, Reversals are everywhere. Stardom and Reversals go hand in hand. Only Adult Heroes can be inspiring enough to reach that level.

In fact, Reversals aren't limited to words. Consider the visual artist Banksy. His images are full of Reversals, making them unforgettable while showcasing Banksy himself as the Adult Hero.

Consider this painting:

The painting itself is a memorable Reversal. The rain is under the umbrella, rather than everywhere else. Similarly, the following image contains an elegant Reversal:

Instead of throwing a Molotov cocktail, the subject is throwing flowers. Banksy takes a common image of opposing authority and reverses just one element.

As you might expect, Banksy's Reversals aren't limited to visual depictions. His famous quotes are full of Reversals. Sometimes, the quotes reverse themselves. He famously wrote, "Art should comfort the disturbed and disturb the comfortable." In both his imagery and his words, Banksy uses Reversals and embodies the Adult Hero archetype.

Previously, we mentioned that Hermione Granger from the *Harry Potter* series is the standard, highly ambitious, highly competitive student. She takes the hardest classes, gets amazing grades in them, tries to follow the rules, starts a community service club (The Society for the Protection of Elvish Welfare). Despite all that, she's just uninspiring. As we mentioned before, she stays in Charted Territory.

In one scene, she beautifully moves through Charted Territory and steps into Uncharted Territory by disagreeing with her professor and the author of her textbook. Instantly, she becomes more inspiring and interesting.

In this scene, the teacher, Dolores Umbridge, is teaching the Defense Against the Dark Arts class. Sadly, she has gutted the class. All practical training has been removed, and the class is now just about reading and memorizing a textbook. The students are told to open the textbook and "commence chapter two."

Here's what happens:

> "I've already read chapter two," said Hermione.
>
> "Well then, proceed to chapter three."
>
> "I've read that too. I've read the whole book."

Notice that Hermione has literally covered all the relevant Charted Territory. She's done all the required research to be ready for this moment. She's at the border between Charted and Uncharted Territory now.

Let's see what Umbridge says next.

> "Well, then, you should be able to tell me what Slinkhard says about counterjinxes in chapter fifteen."
>
> "He says that counterjinxes are improperly named," said Hermione promptly. "He says 'counterjinx' is just a name people give their jinxes when they want to make them sound more acceptable."
>
> Professor Umbridge raised her eyebrows, and Harry knew she was impressed against her will.
>
> "But I disagree," Hermione continued.
>
> Professor Umbridge's eyebrows rose a little higher and her gaze became distinctly colder.
>
> "You disagree?"
>
> "Yes, I do," said Hermione, who, unlike Umbridge, was not whispering, but speaking in a clear, carrying voice that had by now attracted the rest of the class's attention. "Mr. Slinkhard doesn't like

jinxes, does he? But I think they can be very useful when they're used defensively."

First, Hermione covered the Charted Territory. Then, she disagreed with the author of the book and stood up to the teacher everyone hated. She rejected a fundamental view of Slinkhard, the Guide, and presented herself as the Adult Hero, becoming more likeable and inspiring.

These principles of myth are universal and powerful. They have been used to create great stories, great poetry, great literature, great songs, and great comedy. You can use them to create great admissions essays.

They are the most powerful tools to win admissions officers (and everyone else) to your side. You'll use them on personal statements and supplemental essays, and, if possible, in your interviews.

Over the next few weeks, try to notice the Reversals around you. You'll hear them in song lyrics, see them in TV shows and movies, read them in literature, and see them in art. As you become attuned to spotting them, you'll improve your ability to create your own Reversals.

HOW TO CREATE REVERSALS

Reversals are powerful. In one sentence, a Reversal can showcase you as an Adult Hero, the most inspiring of all archetypes. A Reversal can turn an essay from something decent to something incredible. Reversals can help you stand out and get in.

The original masters of Reversals were the Greek Sophists. They would intentionally create ridiculous or absurd views and then find clever ways to prove them. For example, they set out to prove that black was white. They became master rhetoricians through that process. To see a negative view of Sophists, you can see their depiction in Plato's *Republic*. To see a defense of Sophists, you can look at *Zen and the Art of Motorcycle Maintenance*.

But today, we're not going to put Sophists on trial. Instead, we're going to use their mindset to work on some beginner level Reversals.

Most people struggle with Reversals because they want to come up with a view that's "right." For most people, the "right" view is just the commonplace one. In other words, what we see as "right" is absolutely wrong when it comes to Ivy strategy.

A student will start with inspirational quote. The quote represents the Guide. The Guide must be rejected to bring forth the Adult Hero.

Then the student attempts a Reversal…and it's tediously boring. It doesn't showcase the inspiring Adult Hero. It showcases boringness. We see this constantly in our incoming students.

For example, the student might start out with Ronaldo's quote, "Dreams are not what you see in your sleep, they are the things that don't let you sleep." He then reverses it and gets, "Actually, dreams are images you see when you sleep." That's not interesting at all. It's just dull.

There are two things that happened here. First, the original quote is a Reversal. Reversing a Reversal often gets you the common view, which is boring.

INVITATION TO THE IVIES

But the second issue is that the student is trying to be right. The student is trying to be safe. He is trying to say something that cannot be argued against. That deep, fundamental desire for safety creates the boring Reversal.

Even if your starting quote contains a Reversal, you can turn it into another Reversal, if you're willing to step out of the safe zone. For example, you might Reverse Ronaldo's quote by saying, "Ronaldo is wrong. Dreams are what make you sleep."

Charted Territory is safe. Uncharted Territory is unsafe. "Safe" is just another word for "Unheroic." Safe is uninspiring. Safe is not magnetic. Safe is just a guaranteed rejection letter.

If you want to get into an Ivy, you must let go of fear. Bold statements work because they showcase you as the Adult Hero. Fearful and safe statements don't work because they showcase you as an unheroic, frightened child.

Sophists would brag that they could prove that black was white. They didn't worry about the truth; they knew they could come up with clever arguments.

We're going to do the same. Don't worry about what a reversed statement means, or how to defend it. Just reverse it however you like—as long as the reversed position is not a commonly accepted one. After you reverse it, then you can figure out how to defend the reversed position.

Let's start with a few simple, common sayings. The common sayings represent the Guide. Reversing them is the symbolic act of rejecting the guide and presenting yourself as the Adult Hero.

"Don't judge a book by its cover."

This saying reminds us to look past the surface and consider what's below the surface. It reminds us not to judge a person by their physical appearance, for example, but rather to judge them by their character. This saying is good advice that most people would respect. That allows the saying to act as the Guide. For a saying to function as the Guide, it must provide useful guidance. Reversing an incorrect or stupid saying isn't rejecting the Guide; it's just disagreeing with something silly. Reversals only work when they reverse something inspiring or wise.

The two obvious ways to reverse this quote are, "Always judge a book by its cover," or "Don't judge a cover by its book."

At this point, you may be a bit worried. You might be thinking, "Wait, those statements aren't right! How can I argue in favor of them?"

That feeling is good. It's the feeling you're supposed to have.

The most psychologically and emotionally difficult part of a Hero story is when the Hero rejects a view of the Guide. The Guide is her mentor. The Guide called her to greatness. Rejecting one of the Guide's views seems unthinkable. The Hero is nervous thinking it, just as you might be now. But you must.

So, what do we do next? We pick a reversal and find a way to argue it.

Let's go with "Don't judge a cover by its book."

It could be literal—perhaps a graphic designer saying that a great cover is still a great work of art, even if the book inside is bad.

It could be more symbolic, talking about the importance of aesthetics, how the supposedly superficial can be more inspiring and uplifting than what's beneath the surface. For example, it might be someone who didn't like the religion they grew up with, but who was still inspired by its art and architecture.

Let's do another one:

"People who live in glass houses shouldn't throw stones."

One option is "People who live in glass houses should throw stones." Another option is "People who live in stone houses shouldn't throw glass."

Let's go with the first option, "People in glass houses should throw stones." This could be an essay about breaking unstable structures on purpose to allow stronger, better ones to be built. It might be an essay about product design or computer programming. In computer programming, many programmers write their code to fail fast if there is a problem instead of adding protocols that let errors slide. This way, they can find and fix the problem, and create a better program in the long run. Alternatively, the essay might be a story about a person who grew up in a social or cultural environment that he or she didn't agree with, and who intentionally worked to shatter that culture (e.g., someone who grew up in a country in which women weren't allowed to vote).

Let's do another simple one:

"Where there's a will, there's a way."

Let's go with, "Where there's a way, there's a will." This might lead to an essay about how someone might feel stuck if they lack a needed resource (e.g., electricity), not because they lack willpower. It might be an article about a nonprofit that works to bring "ways" to people, thus inspiring them to unlock their own greatness.

Considering common sayings and finding ways to reverse them is a great practice exercise. You might find some that you end up using for a real essay. Even if you don't, it's a great way to develop the mental skills you'll use for other, harder Reversals.

Let's move to the next level of Reversals: reversing famous and inspiring quotes.

This is difficult for two reasons. Of course, it's hard to figure out a way to disagree with something inspiring. But more importantly, many quotes are themselves Reversals. Famous quotes often embody the Adult Hero, and they achieve this by reversing a common view. If you reverse the famous quote, you might end up back at the common view.

Just as -(-5) = 5, a reversal of a reversal is usually just the common, average view.

So, before we attempt to reverse famous quotes, let's go over some common pitfalls.

The first pitfall is a "Reversal to Boring." It happens because the original quote is a Reversal. Reversing that Reversal leads to a boring view. It also happens when you're trying to be too safe.

Consider Scott Adams's Dilbert Principle:

> "The most ineffective workers are systematically moved to the place where they can do the least damage: management."

If you just reverse that without any cleverness, you get, "actually, effective workers get promoted."

That "Reversal" is just a common, obvious, ordinary view. That's not an Adult Hero view. It's not an inspiring view.

The second pitfall is a "Reversal to the Other Side of a Controversy." If you start with a political view shared by half the population and reverse it, you'll likely get a view shared by the other half of the population. That's not a rare, inspiring, Adult Hero view. It's just another common view.

For example, suppose the original statement is, "All guns should be banned." If you reverse it, you get, "No guns should be banned." That's just another equally common view.

Reversing one side of a political controversy without ending up on the other side is a worthwhile challenge. To do it, you have to step into Uncharted Territory, activating the Hero. The results can be clever and unforgettable.

Comedian Chris Rock discusses gun control without ending up on either common side of a controversy:

> "You don't need no gun control; you know what you need? We need some bullet control. Men, we need to control the bullets, that's right. I think all bullets should cost five thousand dollars... five thousand dollars per bullet... You know why? Cause if a bullet cost five thousand dollars there would be no more innocent bystanders.
>
> Yeah! Every time somebody get shot we'd say, 'Damn, he must have done something ... Shit, he's got fifty thousand dollars worth of bullets in his ass.'
>
> And people would think before they killed somebody if a bullet cost five thousand dollars. 'Man I would blow your fucking head off...if I could afford it. I'm gonna get me another job, I'm going to start saving some money, and you're a dead man. You'd better hope I can't get no bullets on layaway.'
>
> So even if you get shot by a stray bullet, you wouldn't have to go to no doctor to get it taken out. Whoever shot you would take their bullet back, like 'I believe you got my property.'"

Instead of just bouncing from one side of a controversy to the other, Chris Rock finds a path in Uncharted Territory. He also disagrees with a prevailing view while rejecting the assumption that there are only two possible sides of this debate. This is one of his most famous standup routines, and it radiates the Adult Hero.

The third pitfall is a "Reversal to Nihilism." This happens when a person doesn't just reject a common view; they reject all life, joy, happiness, and purpose. It's the extreme of throwing out the baby with the bathwater. A Reversal to Nihilism makes you look depressed, depressing, and uninspiring.

Consider this example:

> "The man who says he can and the man who says he can't…are both correct" — Confucius

Reversing this, a student might end up with, "optimists are filled with false hope until they are given a dose of reality while pessimists are those that have given themselves a preemptive dose of reality."

This "Reversal" doesn't insightfully reverse the original quote. It just alerts the reader that the writer has given up all hope and sees reality as a dismal and depressing thing.

The last pitfall is "Agreeing Instead of Disagreeing." You shouldn't do that, obviously. The reversal is the symbolic act of rejecting the Guide. You cannot achieve that by agreeing. But it can happen accidentally when quotes are dense or confusing. With practice, you'll see how to avoid all these pitfalls.

Let's try a quote Reversal. The first step is to find a quote that you agree with and find inspirational. The quote will serve as the Guide, so you personally must find it inspirational. Don't pick a quote you already disagree with. The Adult Hero comes forth when the Hero rejects the Guide, not when he opposes the Villain.

Once you have the quote, try to reverse it while avoiding the common pitfalls (Reversal to Boring, Reversal to the Other Side of a Controversy, Reversal to Nihilism, and accidentally Agreeing).

We'll start with a quote that students often pick for this exercise. Elon Musk said, "When something is important enough, you do it even if the odds are not in your favor."

INVITATION TO THE IVIES

That quote is inspiring. You probably agree with it. That's good news. That means this quote is powerful enough to act as the Guide.

Now, we must reject the quote. The rejection must be forceful and unambiguous.

RIGHT: Elon Musk said, "When something is important enough, you do it even if the odds are not in your favor." Elon was wrong.

WRONG: Elon Musk said, "When something is important enough, you do it even if the odds are not in your favor." This is often true and contains valuable wisdom. However, in some areas, there are aspects that may not be completely accurate.

When you're rejecting the Guide, don't be polite and wishy washy. Don't try to make your view and the Guide's view coexist peacefully. In a hero myth, the death of the Guide is upsetting and traumatic, and it hurls the Hero into adulthood.

Here's what we have: Elon Musk said, "When something is important enough, you do it even if the odds are not in your favor." Elon was wrong.

Now for the tough part: how on earth can that quote be wrong? We could try this:

Elon Musk said, "When something is important enough, you do it even if the odds are not in your favor." Elon missed the point. It's the unimportant things, the ridiculous things, that you should do even if the odds are against you.

This opening seems much better. It also has the nice bonus of being extremely un-dismissive, as it supports the things that others overlook. This opening could serve as an introduction to basically any essay that focuses on your Activity for Fun.

Let's do one more example. Barack Obama said, "If you're walking down the right path and you're willing to keep walking, eventually you'll make progress."

Let's see how we can turn this into a Reversal. We can turn "right path" into "wrong path" and immediately have a nice opening Reversal. Let's see how an opening paragraph might look.

Barack Obama said, "If you're walking down the right path and you're willing to keep walking, eventually you'll make progress." My life has been the opposite. I've learned much more by going down the wrong paths than by clinging to the right ones.

In this case, we personalized the opening a bit more, specifically by talking about "my life" rather than the general principle.

Reversing a prevailing view or inspiring quote can help you present yourself as the Adult Hero, the most compelling archetype.

INVITATION TO THE IVIES

REVERSALS AND COMMERCIAL SUCCESS

Reversals are found throughout commercially successful literature as well as successful Ivy essays. But how do we know that it is the reversals, and not something else, that leads to success?

Let's look at a Forbes book review of Harlan Coben's *Just One Look*. Like most of Coben's books, *Just One Look* got excellent reviews and staggering commercial success. Also, like most of Coben's books, Just One Look is full of Reversals.

Like most reviews of his work, this review in Forbes is overwhelmingly positive. The reviewer pulled just one excerpt from the book. Here's the excerpt the reviewer used:

> "The stages of grief: Supposedly the first is denial. That was wrong. The first is just the opposite: Total acceptance. You hear the bad news and you understand exactly what is being said to you. You understand that your loved one will never come home, that they are gone for good, that their life is over, and that you will never, ever, see them again. You understand that in a flash. Your legs buckle. Your heart gives out. Human beings are not built to withstand that kind of hurt. That then is when the denial begins. Denial floods in quickly, salving the wounds."

Of all the quotes the reviewer could have picked, he chose this clear, dramatic Reversal. The reviewer knew that the book was great and picked out an element that made the book great.

But how do we know the reviewer knew what he was talking about? Who was this book reviewer anyway?

The book review was written by Steve Forbes himself. Steve Forbes is the Chairman and Editor-in-Chief of Forbes media, one of the most influential people in media, and a graduate of Princeton. He knew exactly what elements make writing captivate an audience. Intuitively or consciously, he knew the power of Reversals.

INVITATION TO THE IVIES

REVERSALS AND SONG LYRICS

One way to get good at Reversals is to start noticing them around you. They're everywhere—inspiring quotes, stand-up comedy routines, and religious texts. The Bible tells us, "The meek shall inherit the earth." The Bhagvad Gita says, "One who sees inaction in action, and action in inaction, is intelligent among men."

Most teenagers spend a lot more time listening to music than studying religious texts. Fortunately, popular and successful songs are full of Reversals. In this section we'll look at reversals in a few songs from a few different genres. Soon, you'll be hearing reversals in your own favorite songs.

From Ed Sheeran's "Shiver":
"Baby, you burn so hot
You make me shiver with the fire you got"

From Taylor Swift's "Anti-Hero":
"Midnights become my afternoons"

From Elvis Presley's "Burning Love":
"Burning, burning, burning
And nothing can cool me I just might turn into smoke
But I feel fine."

From Dave Matthews's "Bartender":
"the wine that's drinking me"

From U2's "So Cruel":
"I gave you everything you ever wanted
It wasn't what you wanted."

From Simon and Garfunkel's "Sound of Silence" (note that the title is also a Reversal):

"People talking without speaking
People hearing without listening"

From Billie Eilish's "All the Good Girls go to Hell" (another title that is a Reversal):

"All the good girls go to Hell,
'cause even God herself has enemies."

From Keith Urban's "Wild Hearts":

"All of you lost ones who aren't really lost ones."

From Lil Wayne's "Mr. Carter":

"Blind eyes could look at me and see the truth"

From Bob Seger's "Against the Wind":

"Wish I didn't know now what I didn't know then."

This reverses the common view: "I wish I knew then what I know now."

Over the next months, years, and the rest of your life, you may find yourself hearing more and more epic Reversals in your favorite songs.

Reversals help musicians write hits, help comedians become household names, and can help you write a winning application.

USING REVERSALS TO CREATE PILLARS

Reversals are a great way to create compelling Pillars. We can start with anything, including a big, obvious thing, and use Reversals to create more rare Pillars (which you'll make more complete afterwards).

We'll start by looking at real Ivy League students. The University of Pennsylvania's website has undergraduate student profiles. One talks about a student who got involved in ranching, including competitions and challenges such as "cow cutting, a competition where horseback riders work to separate calves from the herd to within a smaller fenced area."

We can "reverse" that and get competitions and challenges related to vegetable farming…a vegan rodeo if you will. This could be a starting point for anything from an Activity for Fun, which might involve creating physical competitions around veganism, to an Intellectual Mission Statement, which might involve examining the relationship between competition and food in an unexpected way. Those starting points could be developed into compelling Pillars.

Reversals often just alter one critical part of something, just as the Adult Hero dismisses only one view of the Guide. Suppose we start with the Berlin Wall, one of the most famous objects in history. Pieces of the wall are sold as parts of jewelry or as valuable and historical objects. Anything involving the Berlin Wall would obviously be way too common to use.

So, let's "reverse" it a bit. Instead of pieces of the famous Berlin Wall, we might start to think of pieces of other walls that are usually overlooked. Those could be parts of old prison walls, housing project walls, or another disliked wall.

We could "reverse" that further and instead of disliked walls, we could find pieces of beloved objects like parts of old playgrounds. Using that as a starting point, we could continue down a path that no one else is on. This could create great success in any of the Four Pillars.

Keep in mind that starting points are not finished Pillars. The starting point is just something that gets you off the beaten path and into Uncharted Territory. From there, months of research, experimentation, and contemplation will help you develop your initial starting point into a powerful Pillar.

CATEGORIZATIONS

We've talked about Reversals. Reversals are mythologically powerful because they involve the Hero rejecting the Guide and becoming an Adult Hero.

The next of the Three Rhetorical Techniques is Categorization. Categorization is the process of finding differences between two physically identical things. The goal is to find two things that are physically identical but emotionally different.

Reversals are used by poets, comedians, politicians, writers, and leaders. So are Categorizations.

Categorizations are powerful for two reasons. First, they show cleverness and insightfulness. Categorizations require an ability to look at the same object from multiple perspectives, so they showcase intelligence.

The second reason is much subtler. Just as the Hero archetype is so powerful partially because it is formed in infancy, Categorizations are powerful because they are also developed in infancy. This means that they have a deep, psychological impact on people of all ages from all cultures.

Let's look at examples of Categorization so you can get a feel for it. We'll start with an ancient poem, "The Song of Tea," written by Lu Tung:

> The first cup moistens my lips and throat.
> The second cup breaks my loneliness.
> The third cup searches my barren entrail,
>   but to find therein some thousand volumes of
>   odd ideographs.
> The fourth cup raises a slight perspiration;
>   all the wrongs of life pass out through my pores.
> At the fifth cup I am purified.
> The sixth cup calls me to the realms of the immortals.
> The seventh cup - ah, but I could take no more!

I only feel the breath of the cool wind that raises in my sleeves.
Where is Paradise? Let me ride on this sweet breeze and waft away thither.

Each cup of tea here is physically identical but emotionally very different. That's the key to Categorization: you must find the emotional differences between things that are physically identical.

Let's look at a couple of stanzas from a famous poem. It's called "13 Ways of Looking at a Blackbird," so you know it's going to be full of Categories of blackbirds. Feel free to look up the whole poem online:

I
Among twenty snowy mountains,
The only moving thing
Was the eye of the blackbird.
II
I was of three minds,
Like a tree
In which there are three blackbirds.
III
The blackbird whirled in the autumn winds.
It was a small part of the pantomime.

Again, the blackbirds are physically the same. Only the perspective on them changes. They are physically identical and emotionally different.

The poet Robert Graves wrote "The Naked and The Nude," a poem that shows that while naked and nude may appear to be synonyms, they are quite different. According to Graves, naked is good and nude is bad.

Similarly, the show *Seinfeld* has an episode that focuses on the differences between "Good Naked" and "Bad Naked."

Herman Melville's *Moby Dick* depicts Captain Ahab's obsessive search for a white whale (called Moby Dick). In chapter 42, Melville explains that there are two types of white: the nice kind and the scary kind. He goes into considerable depth on this. At one point, he notes:

> "This elusive quality it is, which causes the thought of whiteness, when divorced from more kindly associations, and coupled with any object terrible in itself, to heighten that terror to the furthest bounds. Witness the white bear of the poles, and the white shark of the tropics; what but their smooth, flaky whiteness makes them the transcendent horrors they are?"

Note that Melville compares white to white. He doesn't compare white to off white, ivory, or cream. He showcases two colors that are physically identical…but emotionally different.

A counterfeit painting or gemstone isn't considered good. It's considered criminal and upsetting. While copies may be nearly physically identical to the original, they are emotionally different. In fact, the more similar the copy is to the original, the more we see it as an assault on our reality. The more physically similar the counterfeit becomes, the more emotionally different it becomes.

Categorization can also be applied to commonly conflated terms to highlight their differences. The comedian Chris Rock uses Categorization all the time. He talks about jobs versus careers, rich vs. wealthy, and the like, some of it racially oriented. One famous quote that uses Categorization is, "Shaq is rich. The white man who signs his checks is wealthy."

Categorization is used by writers, leaders, and visionaries. You can use this powerful technique to make your essay unforgettable, make a clever observation, or create a cool theme.

Categorization involves finding the emotional differences between physically identical things. Original art and forgeries may be physically identical, but they are emotionally very different. Holy water and regular water may be physically identical, but they are emotionally very different.

A prop used in your favorite movie may be physically identical to, but emotionally different from, an identical prop not used in that movie. A jersey that was worn by your favorite athlete may be physically identical to (but emotionally different from) an equivalent jersey never worn by that athlete.

A trophy you win might be physically identical to one you could buy from a trophy store, but emotionally very different. If you start a business, the first dollar you earn may be physically and financially identical to the $2,324^{th}$ dollar you earn, but it's emotionally different.

A piece of concrete from the Berlin Wall may be physically identical to a piece of concrete from a random German sidewalk, but emotionally we recognize that they are different.

The second thing that makes Categorization so powerful is that, like the Hero archetype, Categorization also develops in infancy and continues into early childhood.

But how could infants do all this complex differentiation and reasoning? For them, it's completely intuitive.

Infants often get very attached to a particular blanket, pacifier, or toy. When they don't have that object, they can become extremely upset.

This makes things difficult for parents. If an infant loves a particular blanket, then every time that blanket needs to be washed, the infant gets upset during the entire wash and dry cycle. If the infant is attached to a particular pacifier, and that pacifier gets dropped somewhere, then the infant will be upset until it's found.

INVITATION TO THE IVIES 165

Many parents try to out-strategize the infant by simply buying multiple copies of the object. If the infant likes a particular blanket, they just get two more of the same exact blanket. Same for pacifiers, stuffed animals, etc. Since the objects are literally identical, the adult assumes that the infant won't be able to tell them apart and thus will be comforted by both the original and the copies.

Does it work? Heck no! Somehow or other, infants can tell these physically identical objects apart. And just as intensely as they find the "original" comforting, they find the "copy" extremely upsetting. The two objects are physically identical…but emotionally different.

Master horror writer Stephen King understands how powerful Categorization is. He claims that there are three types of terror. Here's what he says:

> The 3 types of terror:
>
> The Gross-out: the sight of a severed head tumbling down a flight of stairs, it's when the lights go out and something green and slimy splatters against your arm.
>
> The Horror: the unnatural, spiders the size of bears, the dead waking up and walking around, it's when the lights go out and something with claws grabs you by the arm.
>
> And the last and worst one: Terror, when you come home and notice everything you own has been taken away and replaced by an exact substitute. It's when the lights go out and you feel something behind you, you hear it, you feel its breath against your ear, but when you turn around, there's nothing there…

The replacement of everything you own by an exact substitute hearkens back to the infant's hatred of the identical replacement pacifier. On the surface, it seems that having everything you own replaced by an exact substitute wouldn't be a big deal. But Stephen King knows that it is one of the worst types of terror. Its power derives from its deep roots which go into infancy.

Have you noticed that a lot of fairy tales involve an evil stepmother? That's bizarre. Fairy tales are supposed to be universal stories for all children, but very few children have evil stepmothers.

Psychologist Bruno Bettelheim sheds light on this odd situation. He realized that "evil stepmother" fairy tales are universal because young children often view their biological mother as two people: the "nice" mother and the "mean" mother. The evil stepmother represents the mean version of the real mother.

In *The Uses of Enchantment*, Bettelheim gives an example of a girl who takes it pretty far. He writes:

> "One day in a supermarket this girl's mother suddenly became very angry with her; and the girl felt utterly devastated that her mother could act this way toward her. On the walk home, her mother continued to scold her angrily, telling her she was no good. The girl became convinced that this vicious person only looked like her mother and, although pretending to be her, was actually an evil Martian, a look-alike imposter who had taken away her mother and assumed her appearance. From then on, the girl assumed on many different occasions that this Martian had abducted the mother and taken her place to torture the child as the real mother never would have done."

What's interesting is that most kids categorize their mother into two separate beings. Bettelheim indicates that "…all young children sometimes need to split the image of their parent into its benevolent and threatening aspects to feel fully sheltered by the first." That's what makes the evil stepmother archetype so universal. To a young child, the angry and kind mother seem to be essentially two different people. They are physically identical…but emotionally different.

Categorization's power goes beyond cleverness. Because of its roots in infancy and further development in early childhood, it is a fundamental process of the human psyche.

The stepmother archetype, by the way, is used heavily in science fiction, fantasy, and literary fiction. In science fiction this is often achieved by having an alien force take over the mother character. (For example, in one episode of *Star Trek: Deep Space Nine*, the mother figure, Keiko, is overtaken by a malevolent alien.) In literary fiction this can be achieved by having alcohol, drugs, or mental illness somehow take over the mother figure. (For example, in *A Long Day's Journey into Night*, the mother figure is a morphine addict, and the morphine addiction leads to the "evil mother" figure.)

In fact, this principle extends into religion. In Hinduism, for example, the kindly Goddess Parvati can take on the terrifying incarnation, Kali. Parvati is the epitome of nurturing gentleness. Kali is usually portrayed holding a severed head and wearing a necklace of additional heads. The two aspects of the same goddess, one terrifying and one nurturing, shows the spiritual and primal power of Categorization.

Categorization continues through early childhood. Children constantly see emotional differences in physically identical things. Consider, for example, what happens when a young child drops an ice cream cone. The parent offers to buy the child another one.

Is the child relieved and grateful? Nope. Usually, he points at the one on the ground and says, "I want that one!" To the child, the original ice cream cone is emotionally different from the physically identical replacement.

Similarly, young children often insist that food tastes better when served in a particular container, that milk tastes better in the blue glass than in the chemically identical green one. This is referred to as "magical thinking," and is a standard phase of childhood development.

Categorization is powerful because it is such a significant part of childhood. The earlier something develops, the more psychological power it has. The Categorization developed in childhood continues to have a profound effect on adults, including the adults who are going to read your application.

USING CATEGORIZATIONS IN YOUR STRATEGY

The most common use of Categorization is just creating cool sentences inside of an essay. Adding Categorizations anywhere in a college essay can help the essay. As a nice bonus, they can help create a memorable conclusion to an essay.

But Categorizations can also be used to create starting points for Pillars.

You can pick any random object. In this case, we'll choose blueberries. We need to find two types of blueberries that are physically identical and emotionally different.

You may be thinking something like, "Maine Blueberries vs. Michigan Blueberries." But those are not physically identical. They are different strains. When students pick two things that have some differences between them, they end up fixating on the minor physical differences, and miss the big emotional differences. The goal is to find the emotional differences, not the tiny physical differences.

There are plenty of options. You might compare the blueberries used for snacks to those used to decorate cakes. You might compare blueberries that are inside of stores to the ones that are for sale right outside of stores. Whole Foods, for example, usually has blueberries for sale both inside and outside. They are the same thing, just in different locations. You might compare blueberries you eat in the morning to blueberries you eat at night. The list is endless.

We're going to pick the second option—comparing the blueberries that are stacked outside the store to the ones stacked inside the store. The idea is you're supposed to buy the ones stacked outside, but Arvin (and most people he observes) buys the ones inside. The ones outside feel more romantic, but the ones inside feel more insect-free.

So, what can we do with that? We might use it as a basis for an unexpected analogy. Something like this:

> My local grocery store stacks blueberries outside for sale, but also sells identical blueberries inside. You're supposedly being enticed to buy the blueberries stacked outside…but everyone walks past the ones displayed out in "nature" (the parking lot), and grabs the ones in the climate-controlled, insect free, unromantic indoor display. That's how I read the newspaper. The front-page headlines are just a distraction. To find what matters, you need to walk past the flashy display, into the humdrum interior pages.

Let's see how we can extend this idea into an Intellectual Pursuit for Fun or Intellectual Mission Statement. This blueberry situation involves decision-making along with a kind of reverse psychology. It involves people looking past the big, official showy things and looking at the inner, subtler things. However, in the case of the blueberries, the outside and inside blueberries are the same, sold by the same company. No matter which blueberries get sold, the same store wins.

That parallels the concept of "controlled opposition" in politics. This is when the dominant party and the opposing party are controlled by the same interests. So, we might use "controlled opposition" as a starting point to develop one of the Four Pillars.

Let's do another example. Let's start with footballs. We can consider the difference between a football used in a championship football game and one used for practice. The championship football is physically identical to and emotionally different from the one used in practice.

We could use this idea as a basis for a memorable analogy. "I felt like a football that has been used in practice but never in a championship game: worn out but untested."

We can then extend this idea to a pillar. We might start by considering the differences between the psychological stress of a daily grind versus the psychological stress of high-pressure situations (e.g., war). We could initially determine the current level of that research, and then narrow down the focus once we had built sufficient expertise. Finally, once we had the needed expertise, we could find a way to push that into Uncharted Territory.

Note that Categorization can bring you to a starting point that leads to an effective Pillar but does not usually produce the final idea right away.

Now let's use Categorization to go into the most Uncharted of all territories, the place where even the boldest people rarely work up the courage to explore: your own mind.

INTRIGUING INTROSPECTION

There are many types of intelligence, and many types of genius. One of the most important types in writing college essays is emotional self-awareness. The ability to have insights into your own emotions shows intelligence, maturity, curiosity, and courage. Most importantly, our own minds are full of Uncharted Territory. As Immanuel Kant put it:

> "Human reason, in one sphere of its cognition, is called upon to consider questions, which it cannot decline, as they are presented by its own nature, but which it cannot answer, as they transcend every faculty of the mind."

Introspection is tough, and most people hate dealing with their own emotions. When you're writing an essay, the last thing you probably want to do is to sit around and think about your emotions. In fact, you might not even want to have emotions.

A few years ago, we created a way to simulate emotional introspection without the bother of doing real emotional introspection. It started with a quote from renowned author and Brown graduate Jeffrey Eugenides:

> Emotions, in my experience, aren't covered by single words. I don't believe in "sadness," "joy," or "regret." Maybe the best proof that the language is patriarchal is that it oversimplifies feeling. I'd like to have at my disposal complicated hybrid emotions, Germanic train-car constructions like, say, "the happiness that attends disaster." Or: "the disappointment of sleeping with one's fantasy." I'd like to show how "intimations of mortality brought on by aging family members" connects with "the hatred of mirrors that begins in middle age." I'd like to have a word for "the sadness inspired by failing restaurants" as well as for "the excitement of getting a room with

a minibar." I've never had the right words to describe my life, and now that I've entered my story, I need them more than ever.

Try to think of a few types of happiness. Here are a few examples to get you started:

- the relief of finding keys that have been lost for more than a day
- the happiness of deciding to order dessert at a restaurant
- the joy of discovering your favorite book has a sequel
- the joy of finding a bag of pretzels in your backpack

If you try to use just one type of happiness to describe something, it can kind of work. But it doesn't have as much power as we want. For example, you might say, "When I decided to enter the race, I felt the joy of daring to do something unfamiliar." But, that's just boring. To give it that sense of emotional self-awareness, we can add in a bit of Categorization… along with a Reversal.

If you decide to enter a race, the type of happiness might be anticipation of something unknown, pride at your own courage, triumph at overcoming fear, etc. It would be very different from the joy of discovering your favorite book has a sequel, or of finding a bag of pretzels in your backpack. So, let's do a Reversal and indicate that the emotion is the opposite of the normal one.

"When I decided to enter the race, the joy I felt had nothing to do with the pride of overcoming my earlier hesitation. It was more like the joy of discovering your favorite book has a sequel."

We just applied a mathematical formula…but it looks like emotional self-awareness. That sentence has the feeling of an introspective, successful Ivy essay.

You can do this with anything but be careful that you don't accidentally sound like a psychopath.

WRONG: "When my grandma died, I felt not the sadness of losing our conversations, but rather the irritation you feel when your computer needs some pointless update."

RIGHT: "When my grandma died, I was struck, not by the sadness of losing the person who had been my real parent, but by the sudden shock that I would have to carry our shared memories by myself."

Make sure the emotion you didn't feel is something that a normal person would expect you to feel. The thing you reject must be the norm.

WRONG: "When I finally mumbled out my speech, I felt not the happiness you feel when you eat a bucket of chocolate, but rather the relief you feel when your phone is fully charged."

No one expects you to feel that stuffed kind of satisfaction after mumbling out a speech. A description like that looks deranged.

RIGHT: "When I finished mumbling out my speech, I felt not the relief of completing a hated task, but rather the excitement at finding the first clue in a treasure hunt."

PRACTICING CATEGORIZATION

You will interact with hundreds of items every single day. As you interact with them, think about how they could be emotionally different.

A lot of this just means asking yourself "How would I feel about this item if I were in a different mood or under different circumstances?"

- How do you feel about breakfast when you're happy vs the same breakfast when you're stressed or rushed?
- How do you feel about your schoolwork the day it's assigned vs the day it's due?
- How do you feel about rain when you're sleeping vs that same exact type of rain when you have a soccer game?

You can also think about counterfactuals, other possible realities that didn't happen but could have.

- How would you feel about rain if you had been experiencing a drought instead of weeks of rainfall?
- How would you feel about coffee if you liked it instead of disliked it? Or if you disliked it instead of liked it? What if you still loved the smell of coffee, but you couldn't stand the taste? What if you worked in a coffee shop and didn't like coffee? What if you grew up in a Mormon town and one day discovered that you love coffee? (Strict Mormons do not drink hot drinks.)
- How would you feel about birds if your dad were an Ornithologist?
- How would you have felt about your piano performance if you had achieved first place instead of second? Or second instead of first?

The last one is a great question because it asks us to confront what we value: either it is the piano performance itself or it is the evaluations of others.

Counterfactuals help us to consider a wide range of possibilities in life instead of exclusively our own experiences.

You can also consider the different purposes or functions of the same item.

- One day, your dog might be there for you to cheer you up. Another day, your dog is there to teach you patience as you try to teach it a new trick.
- Years ago, your matchbox cars were constant play companions. Today, they might be purely decorative and nostalgic.
- Legos easily switch from constructive and exciting toys to pain-inducing foot killers.
- A drone could be used for surveillance or for aerial landscape photography.
- A car tire can be used on a car or chopped up and used as "mulch" at a playground.

Try harder things, too. Like, what could an alternative purpose be for a snowboard? That really seems singularly purposed. Or what about a keyboard? Anything that seems hard, if you think about it for a day or two, will likely turn into something more awesome than the simpler things.

You can also take common items and put them in unfamiliar contexts.

- How do you feel about a Christmas tree ornament at a July 4th party?
- How is a dog toy different when a cat is playing with it? Or when a goldfish "plays" with it?
- How do you feel about flashlights in the daytime?
- How would you feel about a swing set inside of a restaurant?
- How would you feel about lace on a helmet?

You might use some of these exercises in your essays, but more importantly you'll develop the ability to create them as needed.

ANALOGICAL REASONING

The third of the Three Rhetorical Techniques is Analogical Reasoning. Like Reversals and Categorizations, it is used for much more than college strategy. It's used by poets, writers, comedians, politicians, and other leaders.

Analogical Reasoning involves finding similarities between two entirely unrelated things. It is the opposite of Categorization. It may involve finding similarities between lightbulbs and frogs, for example.

Good Analogical Reasoning is seen as proof of high intelligence. In fact, Analogies are part of many standardized tests and intelligence tests.

The larger the gap between the two things being compared, the more the reader perceives intelligence and cleverness. For example, it's easy to find the similarities between crayons and colored pencils. But what about the similarities between, say, ending war and snack food?

The larger the gap between the things being compared, the more memorable the analogical reasoning is.

The most basic type of Analogical Reasoning is just an Analogy. Let's take a look at a few famous examples.

From the movie Forrest Gump:

> "…life is like a box of chocolates. You never know what you're gonna get."

Decades after the movie came out, the analogy helps make the movie unforgettable.

From legendary Secretary of State Henry Kissinger:

> "withdrawal of U.S. troops will become like 'salted peanuts' to the American public: The more U.S. troops come home the more will be demanded."

From world-famous comedian and political commentator, Bill Maher:

> "To most Christians, the Bible is like a software license. Nobody actually reads it. They just scroll to the bottom and click 'I agree'."

From humorist, E.B. White:

> "Explaining a joke is like dissecting a frog. You understand it better, but the frog dies in the process."

Now let's look at a famous Analogy combined with a Reversal. From Jerry Seinfeld:

> "Marriage is like a game of chess, except the board is flowing water, the pieces are made of smoke, and no move you make will have any effect on the outcome."

The first part is the Analogy, and the second part is the Reversal. Notice that the Analogy isn't that clever. "Marriage is like a game of chess" is just obvious. But the reversal makes the quote unforgettable.

Analogical Reasoning is the toughest of the Three Rhetorical Techniques. That makes it the most effective way to showcase intelligence.

Consider this: if a car salesman wants to sell a high-performance car, he doesn't say, "This car is really fast and handles well. If you drove it, you'd see how fast it was. Man, it's fast." Instead, the salesman just asks if you want to test drive it. He knows that a high-performance car will speak for itself.

Similarly, a successful application doesn't say, "I'm really smart. If you would just let me in, you'd see how smart I am." Instead, it demonstrates intelligence within the essays themselves. Analogical Reasoning helps you do that.

So, how do we create Analogies? The first way to go about it is to start out with two completely unrelated things. Let's pick "dogs" and "forks." Go ahead and try to come up with similarities.

At this point, most people make the same mistake. They find similarities that would apply to 99.99% of things. For example, they might say, "Dogs and forks are both objects." True, but so is everything else. They might say, "Dogs and forks can both be seen." That's also true of basically everything.

Analogical reasoning should reveal something non-obvious. Thus, similarities should apply to the two things being compared but not to everything in the universe.

We want to think of things that apply to only dogs and forks, not to everything in the world. We need to start to notice details. Perhaps you notice that both have four "legs" (forks have 4 tines). Perhaps you notice that they have metal structures (dogs have calcium in their bones, and calcium is a metal). Perhaps you notice that both represent civilization. Dogs are domesticated animals, and eating with cutlery is considered more civilized than just thrusting your face into a bowl of food (like a dog).

What do we do with this information? We might use it to create a theme for a book. You might write about the development of symbols of civilization in a more insular empire like ancient Egypt vs a more exposed empire like ancient Mesopotamia. On the other hand, we might just use it to create a memorable turn of phrase: "My morning begins with four-legged inconveniences: my dog and my fork."

PRACTICAL USES OF ANALOGICAL REASONING

The best use of Analogical Reasoning is in explanations. Whenever you're talking about something interesting, complex, or subtle, consider using an Explanatory Analogy.

Suppose you're describing something technical. Here's the boring way to do it:

"I connected the C3 connector to the 4M connector, which increased the memory capacity but reduced processor speed. This allowed it to perform certain tasks, but not others."

Borrrrring.

Here's a better way to do it:

"The new setup increases memory capacity but lowers processing speed; it's like turning a tiny speedboat into a gigantic barge."

Whenever you're describing anything that someone might find boring (basically anything either academic or technical), try using a simple analogy to illustrate your point. The analogy should be simple and unrelated to the original situation. In other words, don't compare one part of cell biology to another part of cell biology. Instead, use a sports analogy, a politics analogy, an animal analogy, or something else simple and relatable.

In an Explanatory Analogy, you be explaining something that people aren't already familiar with. For example, here's how we might explain macrophages:

"The immune system has macrophages. They are like big bouncers outside a nightclub. Also, the bouncers eat you." That's a useful, simple analogy, and it's a little humorous.

"Computers produce color by adding light, like adding toppings to a pizza. Paints produce color by subtracting (absorbing) light. If paints were going to make a meal, they would go into a grocery store and eat everything in the grocery store except for the ingredients that you need." The shift from real color to digital color is quite strange to think about and a cool potential theme for an essay.

Star Trek is one of the most successful media franchises of all time. *Star Trek* skillfully brings in plenty of made-up technobabble without losing the audience. One of its secrets is Explanatory Analogies. When they explain something technical, a character usually follows up with a simpler Analogy. Here's one of many examples from *Star Trek: Voyager*:

> **Torres:** So the antimatter on the ships wasn't duplicated. Both engines have been trying to draw power from a single source of antimatter.
>
> **Janeway:** Like Siamese twins linked at the chest, with only one heart.

Here's one more example:

> **Tuvok:** If we modulated a positron beam to a subspace frequency, it would trigger a thermochemical reaction in the sirillium.
>
> **Sulu:** Like tossing a match into a pool of gasoline.

Even when dealing with a science fiction audience, the very people most likely to be able to follow the scientific explanations without help, Star Trek still uses explanatory analogies. It makes the show relaxing to watch, rather than mentally taxing. It also helps those moments stick in the audience's minds.

Your audience, on the other hand, is probably not going to include many science majors. Application readers tend to be humanities majors since science majors often get higher paying jobs in other areas right out of college. Thus, it's even more important for you to include those Explanatory Analogies. Your essay should be enjoyable and engaging, not a slog through mountains of technical boringness.

Explanatory Analogies are very easy to add in. Every time you start to explain something complicated in math, science, psychology, anywhere, you should think about using an Explanatory Analogy.

Many of our students do math or science research or become interested in highly nuanced things. If your writing gets too dense, add in an Analogy.

The second big way we use Analogies is to show opinions. They're just creative, flavorful ways of expressing how you feel.

"That first project was like a glass of water after a long run on a dry, summer day. This second project was feeling more like a glass of water when you're dripping wet and just choked on pool water coming down the waterpark slide." (Notice we threw in a fun categorization there, too!)

At this point, you know that your instrument or varsity sport probably won't affect your admissions chances at all. But you can use highly specific, nuanced aspects of those common activities to create cool Analogies about your strategic Pillars.

For example, if you play the flute, you might say something like, "The delicate flute takes more air to play than the mighty tuba. Similarly, I learned that the darkest colors in virtual reality simulations, the ones that produce the least light, take the most processing power." (In this case, the strategic Pillar would involve creating a virtual reality simulation. The flute was the common activity, used to create an Analogy to enhance the strategic Pillar.)

Here's another example: "Among the big three watch companies (Patek Philippe, Audemars Piguet, & Vacheron Constantin) Patek Philippe is the king. Vacheron Constantin is like the old, previous king. And Audemars Piguet is the young, upstart prince…"

This is a common opinion in the watch community. But when you apply that to an unrelated topic, you could get an uncommon analysis.

"…The myth is that the same is true in punk poetry. Dadaism is the old king, punk rock is the current king, and punk poetry is the upstart prince. But the reality is that punk poetry and dada are like twins separated at birth, and punk rock is their enemy."

Directly stating opinions in essays usually makes the author look like someone with more ego than intelligence. But, using Analogies, your opinions now sound like insights, and your essay as a whole looks more brilliant.

ANALOGICAL REASONING AND THE FOUR PILLARS

Analogical Reasoning can help you create everything from an Activity for Fun to an Intellectual Mission Statement. Here's how:

First research any topic enough to find something interesting about it. The obvious place to start is any professor's research.

Then, apply that specific idea to a completely unrelated area. For example, if you find something cool about Chemistry, don't apply it to Physics. Apply it to English literature, card games, international law, or something else that has nothing at all to do with Chemistry.

The hardest part is the first part; reading and understanding a professor's thoughts and research is tough. But it is necessary to understand the specifics.

Here's what you get when students don't do the actual hard work of understanding what a professor is saying:

"Professor Q does research on nanotechnology, including different ways to do it. So I thought, why not try different ways to do poetry?"

That's not interesting at all. That's just the definition of writing poetry.

Analogical Reasoning works only on specifics. If you apply Analogical Reasoning to general ideas, you'll get something pointless and boring.

Let's do a few examples. We'll start with a few professor's ideas, understand them well, and then apply them elsewhere.

Completely at random, we start with Stanford Professor Kenneth Schultz. His brief bio has nothing specific enough. However, it does refer to the title of his book, and we can find a PDF online.

There is a nice paragraph that discusses the concept of credibility when countries make threats about war:

> "Credibility is at a premium precisely because states' willingness to carry out their threats is inherently suspect. There are two related reasons why this is so. The first is that carrying out a threat to

wage war is costly. Once called upon to do so, the threatening state might very well decide that the potential benefits of getting its way in the dispute do not, in the end, warrant the costs and risks associated with war. Unless the stakes are great and the costs of fighting small, it is often cheaper to make a threat and back down than it is to wage war. If, however, the stakes and costs are such that it does make sense to fight in the face of resistance, it may still be difficult to convince the target of this fact. This gets to the second reason that credibility is problematic: states have incentives to lie (Fearon 1995). The conflict of interests inherent in crisis situations means that states have incentives to exaggerate their resolve in the hopes of getting the other side to back down."

So now we're going to take this specific concept of credibility and apply it to the most radically unrelated area possible. We're not going to apply it to any obvious area, like economics or law. If you did that, you'd end up with obvious things that are already studied. Credibility is already heavily studied in economics, specifically in game theory, and it is the heart of every type of legal negotiation.

Instead, let's move to the extreme opposite area: molecular biology. We can start thinking about how cells choose to believe or not believe DNA data. For example, are there mechanisms that let those enzymes recognize human DNA as credible, and viral DNA as non-credible? And if not, could such mechanisms be created? At this point, we have a starting point for an Intellectual Mission Statement. Refining it would still take weeks of research, and developing it would take years. Intellectual Mission Statements cannot be done well at the last minute; start in 9th grade or earlier.

Let's take this idea of credibility over to an Intellectual Pursuit for Fun. Let's talk about something that has nothing at all to do with international diplomacy. How about puppet shows? We can start to ask what makes a puppet appear "credible" or not. Exploring why some odd-looking puppets appear trustworthy and other don't could be used to create outlandish but believable puppets could be a starting point for an Intellectual Pursuit for Fun.

Before you dismiss that as a silly plan, consider the amount of thought, research, and development Microsoft put into developing a credible but ridiculous looking digital puppet, Clippy (the famous digital assistant that looks like a paper clip).

How about an Activity for Service? We might start to ask if there are specific groups that suffer because of a lack of perceived credibility, and work on programs to address that. That could be a starting point for creating a compelling Activity for Service.

Finally, let's try an Activity for Fun. You have to be careful with this one, because so many Activities for Fun already play with the ideas of credibility and bluffing. Most card games, many board games, and plenty of video games use these ideas. Bluffing is also a part of nearly every sport.

Thus, we should consider an Activity for Fun that has nothing at all to do with credibility. Dance is not an area in which credibility is usually a focus. Creating a theory of what it means for a dance to be "credible" could be a great Intellectual Pursuit for Fun, and then creating dances that are either more or less credible could be an unusual Activity for Fun.

Let's do one more. This time, we'll start with Yale chemistry professor Sharon Hammes-Schiffer. One of her research focal areas (Intellectual Mission Statements) involves enzyme motion in catalysis. Here's the abstract of one of her major papers:

> "This review examines the linkage between protein conformational motions and enzyme catalysis. The fundamental issues related to this linkage are probed in the context of two enzymes that catalyze

> hydride transfer, namely dihydrofolate reductase and liver alcohol dehydrogenase. The extensive experimental and theoretical studies addressing the role of protein conformational changes in these enzyme reactions are summarized. Evidence is presented for a network of coupled motions throughout the protein fold that facilitate the chemical reaction. This network is comprised of fast thermal motions that are in equilibrium as the reaction progresses along the reaction coordinate and that lead to slower equilibrium conformational changes conducive to the chemical reaction."

To put it in normal English, the small motions in the enzyme help the chemical reactions. Normally, the overall shape of the enzyme is seen as what catalyzes reactions; she is arguing that its small motions are critical.

We can take this idea that "small motion matters more than large structure" and apply it to completely unrelated areas. We're not going to go to biology or physics. Let's take this all the way to cultural communication of social status.

As an Intellectual Mission Statement, we might consider a study of what types of subtle gestures and microgestures indicate different types of status, and how those come to be. For example, are high status gestures just the ones associated with the dominant group? Or are some aspects of gestures high status, regardless of culture?

An Activity for Service might use that knowledge in a training program for a disadvantaged group, or as a cultural training program for hiring managers who want to avoid making biased decisions.

Keeping the idea of "small motions matter more than big structure," see if you can come up with your own Activity for Fun and Intellectual Pursuit for Fun ideas.

By taking something highly specific from one area, and applying it to a completely different area, you can create amazing Pillars.

Note that when generating Pillars, you never end up mentioning the source of the analogy in your essays or applications. For example, if you were talking about gestures, you would never mention the small motions in enzymes. Instead, you would talk about discovering that small gestures can hold people back or help them and then researching gestures more deeply. This way, the Pillar seems driven by an authentic passion combined with close observation of a problem, rather than just a rhetorical trick.

The Unity of the Three Pillars

You may have noticed something about Analogies and Categorizations: they are types of Reversals.

With an Analogy, the common view is that the two things are unrelated; the Analogy reverses this and shows that they are connected.

Conversely, Categorization reverses the common view on two similar or identical things and shows that they are in fact totally different.

Reversals, Analogical Reasoning, and Categorizations all showcase the Adult Hero archetype by rejecting the Guide (the common view).

REVERSALS, ANALOGICAL REASONING, AND CATEGORIZATION IN INTERVIEWS

Reversals, Analogical Reasoning, and Categorizations can help you take your interviews to the next level.

These techniques are most useful when answering follow-up questions, rather than when answering the initial question on a topic. Here's an example of how to do it correctly:

Interviewer: If you could meet any historical figure, who would you meet?

You: I would like to meet Voltaire.

Interviewer: Why Voltaire?

You: I see Voltaire as two people. He is the philosophical and literary giant, but he is also the unknown artist. I would want to ask him how those two different versions of himself managed to coexist.

By using a Categorization in your follow-up, you come across as thoughtful. On the other hand, if you try to put a Categorization in your initial answer, it can seem a bit addled. It might look like this:

Interviewer: If you could meet any historical figure, who would you meet?

You: I would like to meet Voltaire, whom I see as two people. He is the philosophical and literary giant, but he is also the unknown artist. I would want to ask him how those two different versions of himself manage to coexist.

Note that it's not terrible, but it doesn't land as well as using the Categorization in the follow-up discussion.

Instead of a Categorization, you can use an Analogy.

Interviewer: Why Voltaire?

You: Voltaire was like an automobile transported back in time to before there were gas stations. He is an incredibly powerful thinker who didn't have the kind of modern dilemmas that we have today to fuel his thoughts. I would want to know what he thought about _____ and _____.

You could also use a Reversal.

Interviewer: Why Voltaire?

You: Most people see Voltaire as an Enlightenment Philosopher. But I think that at heart, he was really a Dadaist.

Categorizations, Analogies, and Reversals help you answer follow-up "why" questions. Let's do a few more illustrations:

Interviewer: Why would you spend your lottery winnings creating a new type of violin?

Categorization Answer: The violin is really two things. On one hand, it's a creator of melody. But it is also like a keyboard for a kind of pre-linguistic communication. Even infants who can't speak respond to it." (Note that this answer also contained an Analogy.)

Analogical Reasoning Answer: "The violin is like the Speaker of the House of musical instruments. It's not the loudest, but it determines what actually happens in a song."

Reversal Answer: "The violin is not an instrument; it is a piece of communication technology, like a computer keyboard. We've barely scratched the surface of what it can do.

Interviewer: Why do you like writing limericks?

Categorization: There are two kinds of limericks. Some limericks are there to entertain and distract you. Others are there to remind you to look at the parts of the world you've been ignoring. I like the second kind because it reminds me of what I've been overlooking.

Analogy: Limericks are like Phillips head screwdrivers. They are precisely designed to fit only one type of situation, but that's the kind of situation you see 99% of the time.

Reversal: Limericks aren't poems or jokes. They're short stories. I love the idea of fitting an entire story into just a few lines.

The key to using the Three Rhetorical Techniques in interviews is to first practice using them outside of interviews. Try using them in conversations with parents and friends. You can also use them in informal online debates. Online debates give you a bit more time to create answers that use them. At first, each one may take a few days. Soon, you'll be able to generate them much more quickly.

You can also see live examples by watching stand-up comedy. Most successful comedians use the Three Rhetorical Techniques frequently and watching them do it can help you develop your own way of bringing them into your conversations.

Comedian Ricky Gervais's show *After Life*, a show about a man's emotional struggles after his wife's death, illustrates how to use these techniques well in conversation. The script is full of Reversals, with occasional Analogies and Categorizations thrown in.

Practice using these techniques until you can use them easily in normal conversation and recognize them in TV, movies, and everywhere. Once you can do that, you should be ready to use them in college interviews.

TAKING PILLARS TO THE NEXT LEVEL: THE POWER OF CONTRADICTION

Reversals are powerful; taking them to the next level can be more powerful and allow you to present yourself as a compelling and unforgettable person.

Novelists, playwrights, and screenwriters are often told to write multidimensional characters. Many beginning writers find this request bewildering, since pretty much all characters in every movie are three dimensional (except cartoons, which are two dimensional).

In *Story*, legendary screenwriting teacher Robert McKee explains what a "dimension" is, He writes:

> "Dimension means contradiction: either within deep character (guilt-ridden ambition) or between characterization and deep character (a charming thief). These contradictions must be consistent. It doesn't add dimension to portray a guy as nice throughout a film, then in one scene have him kick a cat."

Contradictions are the next level of Reversal. If Reversals were Pokémon, they would evolve into Contradictions. Or, to use a calculus analogy, Contradictions are the limits that Reversals approach.

Superficial Contradictions are the easiest, and they work better than you'd expect. If you create an extracurricular that doesn't stereotypically fit with your gender, body type, or ethnicity, it will make your application more compelling. An Indian girl who pursues rap will seem more compelling than an Indian girl who does Indian dance, for example. A ripped, 300-pound, 6'6" behemoth who writes about creating microscopic art will be more compelling than one who writes about lifting weights. On the other hand, a tiny person who lifts weights or competes in strength competitions could be compelling.

Deep Contradictions are much tougher to do, but their presence can create a profoundly and powerfully nuanced voice. Characters with deep Contradictions become legendary, capture the imagination, and withstand the test of time. Let's see what McKee says about one highly complex character:

> "Consider Hamlet, the most complex character ever written. Hamlet isn't three-dimensional, but ten, twelve, virtually uncountably dimensional. He seems spiritual until he's blasphemous. To Ophelia he's first loving and tender, then callous, even sadistic. He's courageous, then cowardly. At times he's cool and cautious, then impulsive and rash, as he stabs someone hiding behind a curtain without knowing who's there. Hamlet is ruthless and compassionate, proud and self-pitying, witty and sad, weary and dynamic, lucid and confused, sane and mad. His is an innocent worldliness, a worldly innocence, a living contradiction of almost any human qualities we could imagine."

The greatest English writer in history's most famous character is nothing but Contradictions. But you don't need twelve contradictions to make an essay compelling. One or two can set your essays above the competition.

According to McKee:

> "Dimensions fascinate; contradictions in nature or behavior rivet the audience's concentration. Therefore, the protagonist must be the most dimensional character in the cast to focus empathy on the star role."

Similarly, make your application the most dimensional in the stack. Contradictions bring the reader's focus, attention, and empathy to a character. With compelling Contradictions, you can turn the application reader into a fan.

If you don't already do something that contradicts expectations, you can start. Make at least one of your Pillars contradict an expectation that people would have about you. It might contradict your physical appearance or your apparent personality.

You know what's generally expected of you. You know what stereotypes people have of you based on your race, gender, culture, religion, height, weight, anything. Now you can throw off those stereotypes and use that to get into the Ivy League.

Superficial Contradictions are easy to do, and they work. You can find plenty of examples in Harvard Essays published in the *50 Successful Harvard Essays* series. For example, one applicant is African American, but looks like a white girl with blonde hair. Another applicant is a very short boy who rows crew (he's a rower, not a coxswain).

On the other hand, Contradictions between superficial character and deep character are incredibly difficult to do. If you're extremely emotionally self-aware and have put in a lot of work on understanding emotions, traumas, and personality, you might be able to pull it off. But very few professional writers are able to do it, let alone high school students. Even worse, a nuanced Contradiction is likely to be missed by an overloaded application reader.

Focus on the simple, obvious, heavy-handed Contradictions that can make your application memorable and help you stand out and get in.

6

WRITING THE ACTUAL ESSAYS

At this point, you know about the Four Pillars, the Three Archetypes, and the Three Rhetorical Techniques. Now that we have all that framework, let's get more specific about how it all comes together in your essays. The following chapters will look at how to combine techniques for the essays, general writing tactics and tricks to keep in mind, how to think about downbeat essay questions, and how to transform a terrible essay into a good one.

INVITATION TO THE IVIES

REVERSALS + NERD KNOWLEDGE

Writing great Ivy essays involves using your Pillars, Archetypes, and Rhetorical Techniques together. Let's start by connecting Reversals to the Nerd archetype to create possible opening paragraphs for essays.

Previously, we did Reversals with quotes from famous people. Reversals bring out the Adult Hero, the most inspiring of all archetypes. The Reversal is the symbolic act of rejecting the Guide.

How can we bring the Nerd into that? Instead of reversing quotes from famous people…reverse quotes from "Unfamous" people. As a refresher, Unfamous people are those who are famous enough to have a Wikipedia page, but not famous enough to be household names. Just knowing about them demonstrates that prized Nerdy curiosity.

We can start with the example of Alberto Giacometti, mentioned earlier in this book. As a refresher, we picked Giacometti by finding artists from a randomly chosen year. He was the artist who found that when he tried to create realistic sculptures from memory, he ended up creating tiny ones. Let's try to add in a Reversal.

> For 6 years, Alberto Giacometti created sculptures that had a maximum height of 2.75 inches. He said, "But wanting to create from memory what I had seen, to my terror the sculpture became smaller and smaller." As a _____, I've had the opposite experience. As I experience reality from memory, it becomes so large that it's overwhelming.

You would fill in that blank with any title from your Four Pillars. For example: artist, economist, chemist, microbiologist, statistician, salsa dancer, computational biologist, skateboarder, poet, anything.

This Reversal shows Nerd knowledge and the Adult Hero. The only potential issue is that the initial quote has only a small amount of "Guide-ness." It's not exactly advice, but rather just a personal experience. However, reversing it still creates the sense of the Adult Hero. Reversing something other than advice can push you into Uncharted Territory in a nice, subtle way. But for comparison, let's do an example in which we pick a quote that more blatantly represents the Guide.

To start, we'll pick Art as the topic, and we'll use years as a randomization element. We pick the year 1964. The Wikipedia page for art in 1964 talks about some of Picasso's works of that year. It also mentions works by Andy Warhol, Rene Magritte, Jasper Johns, and Norman Rockwell. And then it mentions a bunch of artists that we've never heard of. To project the Nerd, we must pick an Unfamous Artist. In this case, we'll choose Joseph Beuys.

On Wikipedia, we can see that he did performance art, among other types of art. One of his works is "The Chief" which basically involved crouching under a blanket with a microphone for 9 hours. It's the crazy kind of modern art. That will work out just fine.

The next step is to use Google to search for quotes from Beuys. Here's one:

> "Every human being is an artist, a freedom being, called to participate in transforming and reshaping the conditions, thinking and structures that shape and inform our lives."

Notice that this quote has a strong level of "Guide-ness." In other words, it gives advice. Rejecting this view will help us project the Adult Hero. So, let's try an opening that clearly rejects this Guide.

> My favorite performance artist, Joseph Beuys, said, "Every human being is an artist, a freedom being, called to participate in transforming and reshaping the conditions, thinking and structures that shape and inform our lives." Beuys was wrong.

INVITATION TO THE IVIES 199

We made him "my favorite" for three reasons. The first is to make it feel a bit more personal. Personal statements are supposed to be personal. The second reason is to make him feel a bit more like the Guide. For someone to be the Guide, he has to provide meaningful guidance to the Hero.

Finally, we want to throw the audience off a bit; great essays should be full of unexpected moments. Rejecting a view of your favorite artist is unexpected.

Now the challenge is trying to figure out how he was wrong. The quote is pretty inspiring, and when we first look at it, we agree with it. That's good. The Hero starts out agreeing with everything the Guide says.

Our eyes are drawn toward "transforming, and reshaping." Beuys says that artists transform and reshape reality. We can reject that…but it's going to be tricky.

Initially, we want to say something like, "Artists don't reshape anything, they just describe things." But that's not inspiring. The Reversal should be more inspiring than the original, not more depressing.

But maybe we could push that farther to make it work. Maybe "just describing" is good. Perhaps we could argue that artists don't transform reality; they present it, and the audience transforms it. Let's see if that works:

> My favorite performance artist, Joseph Beuys, said, "Every human being is an artist, a freedom being, called to participate in transforming and reshaping the conditions, thinking and structures that shape and inform our lives." Beuys was wrong. Great artists don't transform reality; they showcase reality unflinchingly as it is, then wait for the audience to evaluate and transform it.

It's getting there, but we can do better. Maybe an Analogy could work here. So, we ask ourselves this: who else presents reality? Data scientists, building inspectors, pediatricians, and tailors all measure stuff. Let's try another pass.

> My favorite performance artist, Joseph Beuys, said, "Every human being is an artist, a freedom being, called to participate in transforming and reshaping the conditions, thinking and structures that shape and inform our lives." Beuys was wrong.
>
> Great artists are like data scientists or building inspectors. They don't transform reality; they showcase reality unflinchingly as it is, then wait for the audience to evaluate and transform it.

At this point, we feel there is a usable theme. The idea of waiting feels powerful. It's the opposite of what most people write about. Let's see where that takes us.

> My favorite performance artist, Joseph Beuys, said, "Every human being is an artist, a freedom being, called to participate in transforming and reshaping the conditions, thinking and structures that shape and inform our lives." Beuys was wrong.
>
> Great artists are like data scientists or building inspectors. They don't transform reality; they showcase reality unflinchingly as it is, then wait for the audience to evaluate and transform it.
>
> As a _____, I've struggled to learn to wait for data to transform reality.

And you would fill in that blank with songwriter, martial artist, roboticist, Tik Tok legend, etc.

At this point, this is a usable opening. It showcases the Nerd and the Adult Hero, and thus draws in the reader.

The combination of the Nerd and the Adult Hero is incredibly powerful in Ivy Strategy. It shows passion and intelligence, while creating likability. Your essays and short answers should embody these archetypes from the very beginning and develop them throughout your answers.

DETAILED OBSESSIVENESS

A common student question is, "How can I show talent, achievement, and ability in a compelling way that doesn't just look like the Sociopath?" In other words, how can I show that I'm good at something without just saying, "I'm good at X" or "I won awards in X" or something like that?

To do that, we're going to revisit the two secret powers of the Hero and use them to convey quality. Heroes are insanely persistent and un-dismissive. By showing insane persistence and un-dismissiveness, you can convey quality much more effectively than anyone can with prideful bragging.

Imagine that you wanted to buy a jacket. You're looking at two jackets. One is designed by Paul. The other is designed by Bob.

Here's what fashion insiders say about Paul: "Paul is really passionate about making jackets. Jackets are his major passion, and he makes excellent jackets."

Here's what fashion insiders say about Bob: "Bob is insanely obsessed. He stays up for days just testing out how well different zippers slide, or how they feel in your gloved or ungloved hand. It takes a normal designer about 3 days to design a jacket. It takes him about a year of constant obsession. He once spent an entire month just designing an inside pocket (the one no one ever sees)."

Paul's jackets are probably fine. Bob's jackets are probably world class. They are probably the best jackets ever made.

Notice that nothing positive was said about Bob's jacket. Paul's jackets were called "excellent." All we know about Bob's jackets is that he spent an insane amount of time on every single minor part. He was un-dismissive, as he focused on minor things like zippers. He was insanely persistent.

And that's all we need to know. When Heroic genius is applied obsessively to every supposedly minor detail, the results are invariably extraordinary.

Anyone who creates something great or develops an incredibly high level of skill does so with insanely persistent obsessiveness. Product designers obsess over just one tiny part of a product. Tennis superstars practice one type of serve for months. Basketball pros practice foul shots for thousands of hours.

If you want to show skill or quality, show obsessiveness. Show the details you care about.

But make sure you show the details, not tell them. Don't say, "I care about the details." Instead, talk about the weeks you spent on one tiny piece of a project, or the months you spent on one tiny part of a skill. Describe that tiny task or skill in crazy amounts of detail.

When people care a lot about something, Reversals, Categorizations, and Analogical Reasoning happen naturally. The fictional jacket designer Bob (the crazily obsessed one), could definitely tell you about ten different types of zippers (Categorization). He could also tell you how using one type of material is like using copper pipes for plumbing, and how another type of material is like using PVC pipes for plumbing (Analogical). He could also tell you why his way of aligning pockets is better than the standard way (Reversal).

In your own descriptions of projects you are passionate about, bringing in Reversals, Analogical Reasoning, and Categorizations will convey passion, un-dismissiveness, and Heroic persistence.

AVOID LATINATE WORDS

This chapter looks at one of the most common college essay errors and how to avoid it.

In the early 1900s, novelists William Faulkner and Ernest Hemingway got into a debate in the press.

It started when Faulkner said to a reporter, "Ernest Hemingway: he has no courage, has never crawled out on a limb. He has never been known to use a word that might cause the reader to check with a dictionary to see if it is properly used."

Hemingway's response: "Poor Faulkner. Does he really think big emotions come from big words? He thinks I don't know the ten-dollar words. I know them all right. But there are older and simpler and better words, and those are the ones I use."

One of the most common errors in Ivy essays is overusing big, clunky words. Big, fancy words may get you A's in elementary school English classes, but on Ivy essays they will just make you look stupid. Using big, fancy words makes you look like you're hiding small ideas behind big words. On the other hand, conveying complex ideas or powerful emotions with simple words shows deftness and genius.

The English language has two sources: Latin and Anglo-Saxon. The "advanced" words, like "pulchritudinous," usually have Latin roots. The simple words, like "snake," usually have Anglo-Saxon roots.

Many people wrongly believe that the advanced, Latinate words are better. But really those words have less emotional power. At best, they come across as dull. Usually, they come across as dishonest.

In ancient Rome, after basic education, the children of the elite went on to their equivalent of college education. But their advanced education was different from ours. In America, you can study quite a few different subjects—Chemistry, Literature, Philosophy, Engineering, etc.

On the other hand, higher education in ancient Rome was called "rhetor." Students had two choices: politics or law. You studied to be a politician or a lawyer.

Politicians lie. So do lawyers.

Latin enabled that. Latin can be used as an aloof, distant language, perfect for political dishonesty. In English, Latinate words maintain that aloofness. They lack emotional power, and they tend to lack specificity. When you use Latinate words, you're rarely being specific. Liars hate being specific; they prefer to be as vague as possible, so they can never really be caught in a lie. If everything you say is open to interpretation, it's hard for anyone to prove that you were lying.

Vagueness comes across as dishonesty. Nonspecific sentences jammed with Latinate words come across as dishonest.

Anglo-Saxon words, on the other hand, came from a culture with little or no sophisticated political intrigue. Roman history is full of famous political debates and political deviousness. If you're a *Star Trek* fan, consider the constant political intrigue of the Romulans, a race loosely based on the ancient Romans.

Anglo-Saxon culture was blunter. Compared to Roman culture, Anglo-Saxon culture was barbaric. For our purposes, that's good. Their words weren't devious, political, or vague. They were direct and emotionally powerful.

When Hemingway talks about the "older and better words," he means the Anglo-Saxon words. Those words are the heart of emotionally powerful writing. They are the heart of great writing. They should be the heart of your essays.

At this point, you may say, "Wait a minute! Hemingway used simple words…but Faulkner was also a great writer. Can't we follow his advice, and use the big, fancy words? After all, Faulkner's novels are considered towering works of fiction."

It's true that Faulkner talked about using big words. And it's also true that when Arvin talks to his vegan friends, he sometimes pretends that he eats five steaks a day. He doesn't actually eat five steaks a day, since that would be completely insane.

Faulkner talks about using big words. Let's see if he actually uses them. Here's the opening of *The Sound and the Fury*, Faulkner's most famous work:

> Through the fence, between the curling flower spaces, I could see them hitting. They were coming toward where the flag was and I went along the fence. Luster was hunting in the grass by the flower tree. They took the flag out, and they were hitting. Then they put the flag back and they went to the table, and he hit and the other hit. Then they went on, and I went along the fence. Luster came away from the flower tree and we went along the fence and they stopped and we stopped and I looked through the fence while Luster was hunting in the grass.
>
> "Here, caddie." He hit. They went away across the pasture. I held to the fence and watched them going away.

Did you notice any big words? Of course not. Faulkner might talk about using big words, but he's not crazy enough to use them.

Consider the most famous line in English literature:

"To be or not to be, that is the question."

The power comes from the sheer simplicity of the words along with the power of the ideas. Shakespeare didn't write, "Sometimes it may be necessary or exigent to determine the net intrinsic value of one's own existence."

If he had done that, he wouldn't have been Shakespeare. He wouldn't have been The Bard, the greatest playwright and poet of the era. He wouldn't have been the bestselling writer in the entire English language. He would have just been some guy who got rejected from the Ivy League.

Consider the advice of novelist and creative writing professor John Gardner (author of *Grendel*, among other books.) In *The Art of Fiction*, he writes:

> "A scene will not be…vivid if the language the writer uses is abstract instead of concrete. If the writer says "creatures" instead of "snakes," if in an attempt to impress us with fancy talk he uses Latinate terms like "hostile maneuvers" instead of sharp Anglo-Saxon words like "thrash," "coil," "spit," "hiss," and "writhe," if instead of the desert's sand and rocks he speaks of the snakes' "inhospitable abode," the reader will hardly know what picture to conjure up on his mental screen."

Simple words create emotional power and vividness. Big words just look vague, dumb, confusing, and dishonest. When you're writing and editing your essays, replace those complicated, Latinate words with sharp, simple Anglo-Saxon words every time.

FAVORITE WORD & OTHER DOWNBEAT QUESTIONS

The Adult Hero archetype can obviously be used in big essays, like the Common App personal statement. But it can also be used in many unusual and seemingly unimportant questions. In fact, using the Adult Hero archetype in these downbeat questions is more powerful, since it's unexpected.

For example, colleges sometimes ask, "What's your favorite word, and why?" Let's see how the Adult Hero archetype can help us here. The Hero becomes the Adult Hero when he rejects some important advice of the Guide. When we're talking about a word, one common Guide is the dictionary.

Students approach this essay topic in various ways. Some students pick an intentionally difficult word, like lachrymose (crying easily) or pulchritudinous (beautiful). Other students put a spin on it, by picking a word that is both difficult and highly specific. In other words, they pick a word that doesn't have a simpler synonym.

For example, a student may pick "petrichor," which is the smell of rain on dry soil. There's no simpler word with the same definition. We've recently discussed why such selections might not the best choice; complicated words make you sound like you're hiding small ideas behind big words. But we'll show an example in a moment of how to make it work in this context. (Hint: we're going to reject the complex word.)

Some students, feeling the correct instinct to reject the Guide, choose intentionally offensive words or swear words. Intuitively, they have the right impulse to reject the Guide, but those essays rarely if ever work.

On Bullshit, the *New York Times* bestseller written by Princeton Professor Harry G. Frankfurt, is entirely about one swear word. If you really want to use a swear word, read *On Bullshit* first to understand the level of intellectual quality expected. Very few students can reach that level of intellectual quality in a single, short essay. Even Professor Frankfurt needed an entire book to do it justice.

Usually, the best way to proceed is to pick a small, common word and then bring in the Three Archetypes and the Three Rhetorical Techniques. Let's start with one of the simplest words we can think of: dog. We'll also use the appropriate Guide, which is the dictionary.

Dictionary.com reminds us that dog can also be used as a verb, meaning to follow or track like a dog, as in, "He dogged my steps" or "The private investigator dogged his target." During this brainstorming stage, we are reminded that dogged means persistent, that doggerel is bad poetry (either accidentally bad, or intentionally bad in order to be funny), that "doggone" is a polite replacement for swearing, and that prairie dogs exist. We might use some of these facts, all of them, or none of them.

So, let's put it together.

> My favorite word is "dog," used as a verb. As in, "to follow closely" like a dog. It comes from the fact that dogs relentlessly follow their quarry, or that dogs closely follow their owners.
>
> Except they don't. Leashes prevent modern dogs from pursuing quarry, and most dogs pull at the leash instead of following politely behind their humans. Dogs walk ahead, sometimes anticipating their best friend's intention, usually anticipating their own whims, and frequently pulling at the leash.
>
> That's what "dog" should mean: to pull slightly ahead, like an actual dog. And dogging, using that definition, describes the rarest, greatest, most precious moments of creativity. It's when a brilliant new hypothesis pulls ahead of the scientist supposedly making it, when the story pulls ahead of the author, when the painting is a few steps ahead of the artist's brush, when the design is a step ahead of the engineer. "Doggerel" means bad poetry, but it should

mean the most inspired poetry, the kind that writes itself while the poet catches up.

Dogging is one step ahead of what Mihaly Csikszentmihalyi calls "Flow." It's when a sculpture is already hidden in the stone block, and the sculptor catches up to it. Dogs are man's best friend, but dogging is man's purest expression of love, where the line between the creator and created vanishes, the roles reverse, and the extraordinary creates us.

By repeatedly using Reversals, we can showcase the Adult Hero and create memorable essays. Let's do another. This time, we can start with the aforementioned word "petrichor," which means the smell created when rain falls on dry soil. But this time, let's bring in the Reversal earlier. Instead of using the word "petrichor," We'll replace it with "rain-stank," which is a made-up word meaning less-fancy petrichor.

As usual, we've looked up the word "petrichor" to see if the Guide has something to reject. The word comes from "petra" meaning rock, and "ichor," which means the blood of the gods. (Note that petrichor comes from Greek, not Latin, but suffers the same lack of emotional immediacy and power as Latinate words.) We've also looked up what chemical components make up petrichor.

> My favorite word is "rain-stank." Rain-stank is the common man's petrichor. Compared to petrichor, rain-stank has $1/10^{th}$ the geosmin, $1/100^{th}$ the plant oils, $1/1000^{th}$ the romance, and about fifty times the ozone.
>
> Etymologically, petrichor comes from the Greek "petra," meaning rock, and "ichor" meaning blood of the gods. Rain-stank isn't fancy enough to have an etymology, but if it did, it would come from the Greek word for concrete and the Latin word for "a

mixture of brake fluid, gasoline, sweat, antifreeze, and some other stuff you don't want to know about."

I've experienced petrichor once at my aunt's house. It was incredible. I've experienced rain-stank a few billion times. It's ordinary.

If this seems like I think rain-stank isn't as good petrichor, let me clarify. Petrichor is the smell of divine inspiration. Rain-stank is the smell of human grit, relentlessness, and persistence. It's the smell of will, the smell of getting up again after you've been knocked down, the smell of trying long after everyone has told you to give up. It's the smell of supposedly dying cities in which new businesses still open, the smell of "forgotten" towns where people proudly raise families.

If genius is 99% perspiration and 1% inspiration, then rain-stank is the smell of that 99%. Petrichor may have inspired the idea of the aqueducts, but rain-stank is the toil and perseverance that turned those ideas into stone and cement. If petrichor inspired the idea of touching the moon, rain-stank put human footprints on it.

And rain-stank gives its own inspiration. Petrichor may have inspired Wordsworth, but rain-stank inspires the poets who showcase and transform the ordinary, reminding us to actually see what we're looking at. When the gods forget to inspire us, rain-stank reminds us to inspire each other.

Petrichor is the perfect smell. Rain-stank is as imperfect as the never-ending quest to understand ourselves, to explore the unknown, and to strive beyond inspiration.

With a mix of Reversals and Categorizations, we can create a memorable essay that shows the Adult Hero.

The entire thing is one big Reversal because your "favorites" are expected to be extraordinary things, not ordinary ones.

The entire thing is also one big Categorization, explaining the difference between petrichor (the smell of rain on dirt) and rain-stank (which is also the smell of rain on dirt).

Then we have big analogies talking about what petrichor represents (divine inspiration) and what rain-stank represents (human grit and relentlessness, very Heroic).

We also have a smaller Categorization: the difference between seeing something and looking at it.

When you break it down, it's just Reversal after Categorization after Analogy after Reversal…and so on. This is how you take the mystery out of college essays. This is how you can turn your essays into an equation for Ivy acceptance.

We'll give you another example of a downbeat question: What is your favorite book?

These minor questions seem less important than the big Common App personal statement. They're often physically smaller questions, allowing fewer words, and so the average person tends to think of them as less significant. But these questions are the most revealing. The applicant's guard is down. These downbeat questions "leak" more information than the bigger essays. They reveal more truth.

Most applicants handle this question terribly. Often, students pick books like *The Lion, the Witch, and the Wardrobe* or *A Wrinkle in Time* that basically everyone has read. Obviously, this violates the basic Scarcity Principle. If Yale accepts fewer than 2,400 people a year, choosing a book that 99% of applicants have read is a terrible idea.

But some students do worse! They pick a required reading book from school—something like *To Kill a Mockingbird* or *The Great Gatsby*. Instead of picking a book that 99% of students have read, they pick a book that 100% of students were required to read.

One of our students with a "mathematically impossible" application took a totally different approach. (We call the application "mathematically impossible" because her high school told her there was no mathematical way she could get into her top-choice school, according to their own statistics.)

But she understood the importance of Reversals, and she understood that the Adult Hero archetype is created by rejecting the Guide. In this case, she decided to make the Guide a professor from her dream college. She began the process by trying to find a book that was relevant to her Intellectual Mission Statement that a professor from the university had commented on.

She didn't pick a book that a professor had written. That may have been a bit too obvious. Instead, she picked a book that a professor had just commented on. The purpose was obviously to apply a Reversal to the comment.

In her essay, she briefly introduced her research topic then talked about this book she had found and specified what parts of the book she found compelling. She described the ideas clearly and simply, using explanatory Analogies when appropriate. She then indicated what the professor from the university had said about the book. Then, she intelligently disagreed with the professor. She presented and backed up her argument well. Finally, she talked about her desire to research and debate with that professor.

She got into that college, much to the shock of her high school counselors and her more academically gifted peers (who didn't get in).

Downbeat questions are very powerful. If you think a question is unimportant, then they've tricked you. Every single question is important when you're showcasing a carefully constructed persona.

Ivy applications have plenty of these downbeat questions, which you'll usually answer by using the Three Archetypes and the Three Rhetorical Techniques. Here are a few examples:

- **Dartmouth:** "Be yourself," Oscar Wilde advised. "Everyone else is taken." Introduce yourself in 200-250 words.
- **Dartmouth:** "Not everything that is faced can be changed; but nothing can be changed until it is faced," wrote James Baldwin. How does this quote apply to your life experiences?
- **UPenn:** Write a short thank-you note to someone you have not yet thanked and would like to acknowledge.
- **Princeton:** What is a new skill you would like to learn in college?
- **Princeton:** What song represents the soundtrack of your life at this moment?
- **Stanford:** Virtually all of Stanford's undergraduates live on campus. Write a note to your future roommate that reveals something about you or that will help your roommate—and us—know you better.
- **Stanford:** What historical moment or event do you wish you could have witnessed?
- **Georgetown:** Indicate any special talents or skills you possess.
- **UC:** What would you say is your greatest talent or skill? How have you developed and demonstrated that talent over time?
- **UC:** Beyond what has already been shared in your application, what do you believe makes you stand out as a strong candidate for admissions to the University of California?

Your Pillars might relate to some of these, but these questions are really where the Archetypes and Rhetorical Techniques shine.

We've already talked about how to answer the "what historical moment do you wish you could have witnessed" question: focus on July 4th moments, rather than September 3rd moments. There are other approaches as well.

In his "I've Been to the Mountaintop" speech, considered one of the best speeches ever written, Dr. Martin Luther King Jr. talks about what he would do if God allowed him to pick what time in history he was going to live in. He disagrees with the prompt by asking to live in exactly the time he's already living in. Here's how he showcases the Adult Hero:

> "Strangely enough, I would turn to the Almighty, and say, 'If you allow me to live just a few years in the second half of the twentieth century, I will be happy.' Now that's a strange statement to make because the world is all messed up…But I know, somehow, that only when it is dark enough, can you see the stars…And another reason that I'm happy to live in this period is that we have been forced to a point where we're going to have to grapple with the problems that men have been trying to grapple with through history, but the demand didn't force them to do it. Survival demands that we grapple with them."

That specific answer wouldn't work now since it was already used in one of the most famous speeches in history. But notice that it turns the question on its head, showcases the Adult Hero, and becomes one of the most memorable speeches ever written.

There's no cookie cutter way to answer any of these questions. But there are guidelines that can help.

Use the Three Rhetorical Techniques frequently. Feel free to put in multiple Categorizations, Analogies, and Reversals into a single short answer.

Remember the un-dismissiveness of the Hero and Nerd archetypes. Talk about things that others would overlook. For example, when picking a song for the Princeton application, picking a grandiose or narcissistic song like White Zombie's "More Human than Human" or Daft Punk's "Harder, Better, Faster, Stronger," is not the way to go. Pick a song that lets you showcase the un-dismissiveness that makes the Hero and Nerd so powerful.

Remember the power of Contradictions. Contradictions make the main character (you) more compelling. When introducing yourself, it can be a good idea to start with a contradiction.

When doing this, keep in mind the un-dismissiveness of the Hero. The students who dismiss minor questions get rejected. Stay un-dismissive, focus on the downbeat questions, stand out, and get in.

A TERRIBLE ESSAY (AND HOW TO FIX IT)

A few years ago, we wrote an essay designed to guarantee rejection. We use it to see how well a student has understood the principles of college strategy. If you're understanding this stuff, you'll spot quite a few errors. See how many you can find.

Here's the essay:

> The brush in my hand is now tipped with blue-green paint. I face the blank challenge of the canvas. Confidently, I apply the first stroke.
>
> This isn't my first painting. It won't be my last. But this painting is unique.
>
> I fell in love with oil painting during the summer after my sophomore year. My family was vacationing in our villa off the southern coast of Italy. My parents signed me up for a painting class, and I agreed.
>
> After I finished my first oil painting, I was excited to try more. I signed up for an intermediate class while we visited Venice.
>
> When I got back to school, I signed up for painting, fulfilling a graduation art requirement. As I improved, I was soon getting an A in that class. I even joined my school's art club. I was excited to learn about great artists, like Monet, Picasso, and Dali.
>
> Painting has taught me the importance of hard work and perseverance. Paintings can take hours, and you can't give up, no matter how difficult it gets. Sometimes, painting can be frustrating.
>
> As I apply the final dot of color on the painting, I feel happy that I finished the painting. I look at my work, and I'm proud that I have achieved my goal.

Ouch. That essay is incredibly self-destructive. Go ahead and think about what makes it so bad. Feel free to reread the essay a few times to find the errors.

Here's our analysis.

- The student comes across as incredibly spoiled and privileged. Visiting a family villa, taking art classes in Venice, etc. By the way, this error is incredibly common. Students often do "service trips," which is community service in another country. Students hope that this will make them seem charitable and unique. It only makes them look spoiled and overprivileged.
- The student demonstrates zero initiative. He says that his parents chose the class, not that he begged and pleaded to take the class… or better, chopped wood for a summer, so he could take the class.
- The student shows the worst type of motivations. He takes the class to fulfill a graduation requirement, and then, to make things worse, he shows that he is motivated by grades. He isn't showing that he is motivated by curiosity, passion, excellence, or a desire to push the boundaries of a subject.
- The perseverance level is completely off. Ivy League perseverance is measured in years. The student brags about persevering for "several hours."
- The "perseverance" demonstrated isn't perseverance. The student faces no failures or setbacks. What he's calling "perseverance" is just completing the task.
- The student mentions artists that everyone on earth knows about. He should have picked artists that are not known to the general public, which would have shown curiosity, passion, and real interest.
- There is no emotional introspection at all.

In addition to containing several self-destructive elements, the essay is lacking the following:

- Surprising or unexpected insights.
- A strong personality that goes against a pre-existing belief. In other words, the Adult Hero is absent.
- Any concern for any cause outside of the student's own interests.

And finally, let's consider the topic itself, which is painting.

Stanford lets in less than 2,200 people a year. There are 35,000 schools in the country. Each school has between 20 and 900 people who are interested in art. The topic is a few orders of magnitude away from being usable.

Let's go about fixing this. Here are the principles we're going to use:

- Reject the Guide. That means find a compelling view and then reject it.
- Showcase the Nerd. That means discussing facts that other people don't know about.
- Get into Uncharted Territory to showcase the Hero.

There are two ways to fix this. One option is to add some Reversals, Categorizations, and Analogies to the current essay, like putting ornaments on a Christmas tree. If you put enough ornaments, it might be decent. For example, you might add something like, "I realized that there were two kinds of art classes: the kind that feels like an art class, and the kind that feels like CrossFit. This was the second kind." In that case, we added a Categorization with a Reversal.

Adding elements of the Three Rhetorical Techniques (Categorizations, Analogies, and Reversals) can turn a mediocre essay into a good essay. They can also turn good essays into outstanding essays.

But they rarely transform a mediocre essay into a great essay. With an essay this terrible, the smart move is to throw out the original essay and build a new one. Don't try to put lipstick on a pig; toss out the garbage and make something new.

Let's keep the same overall topic (art), but we'll throw out all the original stuff and rebuild.

We're going to start with the easiest part: finding artists and facts not known to the general public. We're going to keep it simple(ish). First, we'll pick any year at random, and use that to find an artist.

We pick 1915 and try to find an artist that we haven't heard of. We find Isaac Rosenberg. A quick Wikipedia search shows that he is a poet and visual artist. We find his most famous quote:

> "I will not leave a corner of my consciousness covered up but saturate myself with the strange and extraordinary new conditions of this life, and it will all refine itself into poetry later on."

This quote will work. It's compelling and inspiring, which allows it to act as a Guide. Obviously, we plan to disagree with it at some point in the essay.

Rejecting the Guide is the most important moment of any hero myth. So, we're going to start with that.

Rosenberg says he is going to saturate himself with the "strange and extraordinary new conditions of this life." The opposite of that would be to saturate yourself with the common and ordinary parts of life. That feels like it's going to work well. Very few people would choose to say they're interested in the mundane. Most students are drawn to the outlandish and weird. Most people are interested in space, neuroscience, quantum physics, and other exceptional things. Almost by definition, no one is interested in the boring and mundane parts of life.

So now let's to learn a bit more about the artist. Some research reveals that he is more famous as a poet than as a painter. That might work well, since poets are likely to have usable quotes.

Now we can review his artwork. It's serene, sort of impressionistic. Given that he was in World War I, the serenity is unexpected. We notice that in his self-portrait, he looks a bit like Sacha Baron Cohen (the comedian who created *Da Ali G Show* and *Borat*).

The artwork isn't as exciting or lurid as surrealism. That's good, because most teenagers are drawn to surrealism, and approximately zero percent of teenagers would be drawn to Rosenberg's style. The goal is to stand out and get in, not be like everyone else.

Now let's add in a Categorization. Words that describe Rosenberg's paintings might include tranquil, peaceful, boring, mundane, reflective, contemplative. The choice is obvious. We should pick the one that no one would use in a college essay: boring.

So, what are the two types of boring? Something boring puts you to sleep. Let's add in a Reversal and say there is a second kind of boring that wakes you up.

A bit of analogical reasoning won't hurt. Let's pick two things totally at random and see if it goes anywhere. For now, we just look around the room. There is a computer speaker, a paper plate, an aquamarine stone, a pair of safety goggles, a bottle of cleaner, a wallet, a tape measure. The computer speaker and paper plate seem the most unrelated.

What is the same in both of those? They are manufactured. Mass produced. Common. Ignored. Convenient but unnecessary. "Convenient but unnecessary" sounds like the most useful theme, but that might change.

Through this whole process, keep one major thing in mind: stay flexible. Be willing to change anything or everything. Don't get attached to any part of any essay.

As an initial direction, let's go with rejecting the commonly preferred type of art, which, for teenagers, is usually surrealism. It's also preferred among adults. Surrealism is cool because it's all about presenting the unconscious in dreamlike and lurid ways. When we think of surrealism, we might associate it with dream exploration, lucid dreaming, and the like. We start by rejecting this common preference:

> My obsession/love affair with surrealism ended when _____.

What type of event could have caused this change? It could be a gradual falling away. It could be a solitary walk with an epiphany. It could be a conversation.

It must be believable. It shouldn't happen during a shipwreck, since around zero percent of people are ever in shipwrecks.

This moment should reflect human nature. Don't write anything like, "My love affair with surrealism ended when my grandma told me to stop liking surrealism." That's not how humans work.

This moment should reflect useful qualities. Don't write: "My love affair with surrealism ended when it was just too much work, and I didn't want to put all that effort into learning anymore." That just shows laziness, obviously. We want to show curiosity, persistence, collaboration.

> My love affair with surrealism ended while I was working on a surrealist video game.

That feels pretty good. Designing video games shows persistence and a willingness to step outside the standard extracurriculars and hobbies that most teenagers do. It also has an intriguing paradox (falling out of love with surrealism while being involved with surrealism), leaving the audience curious about how that change happened.

The key to drama and suspense is to not give the audience what they want too quickly. Consider a murder mystery. The reader wants to know who the killer was. The author could just tell the reader right away, supposedly giving the reader what he wants. But by giving the reader what he supposedly wants, the author would rob the reader of the experience of reading the mystery.

So, we're not going to give away how the video game creation led to losing interest in surrealism yet. Instead, let's fill in some backstory, designed to showcase curiosity.

> My love affair with surrealism ended while I was working on a surrealist video game.
> For the previous two years, I had been obsessed with the unconscious.

Now we need to do some research. Some of the ways that people get into studying the unconscious is by studying famous psychologists like Freud and Jung. We already know that Jung talks about archetypes, synchronicity, and the collective unconscious. So let's look up contemporary psychologists who work on dreams and the like.

We typed "psychologist dreams" into Google and scrolled through the psychologists at the top until we started seeing ones that we didn't recognize. There's G. William Domhoff, who researches dreams and works on sociopolitical issues, specifically suggesting that America is run by an elite ruling class.

There's also Dierdre Barret, who scientifically researches dreams and lucid dreaming. One of her books is called *The Pregnant Man and Other Cases from a Hypnotherapist's Couch*. That bodes well. If her book has a Reversal right in the title, she'll probably work just fine.

She talks about "supernormal stimuli," which is, according to Wikipedia, "the idea that technology can create an artificial object which pulls an instinct more strongly than that for which it evolved." That works well for the current essay because video games probably involve supernormal stimuli. That feels powerful enough for the essay.

Often, students ask, "What should my essay be about?" The answer is that it doesn't matter at all. Consider the towering works of English literature. Most are about very little. On the other hand, low level entertainment fiction is often about really exciting things—aliens attacking earth, people getting magical powers, etc.

A Catcher in the Rye is a book about a guy who gets expelled from a private school and then wanders around New York for a couple days. It's not about anything particularly dramatic. Hamlet superficially seems to be about something dramatic—a son avenging his father's murder. But the actual play is mostly about Hamlet doing nothing.

College essays are in the literary category rather than the entertainment category. Great essays are made great by their insights and contemplative moments, not by their epically dramatic scenarios.

Similarly, it won't matter at all which specific psychologists we pick. They just have to be psychologists that aren't universally known. They need to be rare enough to showcase the Nerd's curiosity.

Ivy essays aren't built around plot; they're built around insights. So, let's start by listing a few insights, and building the rest of the essay around them.

- My love affair with surrealism ended while I was working on a surrealist video game.
- There are two kinds of boring: the kind that puts you to sleep and the kind that wakes you up.
- Theme: "convenient but unnecessary"

- Isaac Rosenberg said, "I will not leave a corner of my consciousness covered up but saturate myself with the strange and extraordinary new conditions of this life, and it will all refine itself into poetry later on." (Reject this view by focusing on the boring.)
- Nerd knowledge: G. William Domhoff researches dreams and works on sociopolitical issues. He suggests that America is run by an elite ruling class.
- Dierdre Barret talks about dreams and supernormal stimuli.

With that, let's create a sketch of an essay.

> My love affair with surrealism ended while I was working on a surrealist video game.
>
> For the previous two years, I had been obsessed with the unconscious. I had read every book I could find on lucid dreaming and had had a few semi-successful attempts at controlling my own dreams. I had read much of Jung's work. (I read Man and His Symbols a few zillion times.) The dream archetypes he describes would later make their way into the aforementioned video game. Mandalas, which he describes in detail, were used as templates to create the maps of that game. My computer backgrounds were paintings by early surrealists like Dali and Tanguy, as well as modern ones like Ming Ying and Seb Janiak. [NOTE: we looked up the last two. We didn't immediately know any modern surrealists, so we found a couple on Google.]
>
> I was embodying my favorite quote, which came from poet and painter Isaac Rosenberg: "I will not leave a corner of my consciousness covered up but saturate myself with the strange and extraordinary new conditions of this life, and it will all refine itself into poetry later on." My fascination with the strange and surreal led

me to meditation and graphic design, to Dadaist poetry and dream journaling, to holograms and Taoist philosophy, and ultimately to video game development.

Yet, there was something that never quite fit about Rosenberg's quote. He talked about exploring the strange and the extraordinary. But his paintings are of fairly ordinary things: portraits, landscapes, scenes of normal life. There were no melting clocks, magical doors in empty fields, dreamlike nightmares, or shadows and reflections creating bizarre apparitions. I accepted it as a simple paradox; given my own personal contradictions, it seemed unfair to criticize someone else's.

There's an interesting cliche about video game design: game engines spend inordinate amounts of resources to create normal things. It takes more processing power and programmer ingenuity to create realistic fog than to create a surrealistic monster. While working on my video game, I fell deeper into the rabbit hole of learning about the tools that made the realism more real. I also found myself thinking about the dreamlike time in video games where the mundane is removed, compared to the tedium of real time. The more I worked on surrealism, the more I felt sucked into realism.

Rosenberg's paintings started to make sense; the quote about the extraordinary and the paintings of the ordinary seemed less like two discordant parts of a personality, and more the same side of the same coin. When I wasn't working on the surrealist game, I thought about the boring parts of reality that no game had yet captured.

There are two types of boring: the kind of boring that puts you to sleep, and the kind that wakes you up. The ordinariness of

Rosenberg's paintings, which I'd first seen as tranquil, I now saw as crackling with life.

They say all critics secretly want to be artists. I wonder if every surrealist yearns to connect with reality. I wonder where the surrealist's search for hidden truths ends, and where addictive escapism begins. I wonder if, in our exploration of the unseen, we've lost sight of the seen.

I've done more than wonder. I've read the works of Kohler and Fechner in my exploration of perception. I've watched and rewatched films of Michael Haneke that showcase life in real time, rather than in dreamlike film time.

I believe that that which bores can inspire more than that which captures the imagination. Two years ago, I would have wanted to explore the weirdest things possible. If I were going to create a major, it would have been Quantum Philosophy or Time Studies or The Neuroscience of Abstract Art. And if those subjects were offered as individual courses, I doubt even now that I'd be able to resist them.

But for my major itself, I want to explore the mundane, the boring, in a way in which it has never been explored before. I doubt that "Boring Studies" is a major at any university (unless you count Applied Math), so I plan to create a new major that reexamines the mundane. I can't predict where this study will take me, or what paths I'll travel. I plan to start with psychology, the history of science, and the history of art and architecture. I plan to find not what's hidden behind the boring, but what's hidden in the boring itself.

How would we move from an initial sketch to a final draft? We might explore more deeply the ideas of the psychologists mentioned or the art of the painters mentioned. At the moment, they're basically just placeholders. We could add more insights, more emotional nuance, etc. But we have a good starting point that we can add to, instead of junk we need to try to cover with distractions.

Not everything discussed in the initial setup made it to the final essay. That's normal. When you're writing an essay, you don't need to fit in every part of your notes into the draft. Some things won't fit; other things you haven't thought about will be needed to fill in gaps. For example, we had to look up modern surrealists to fill in gaps in the narrative.

Your first drafts may not look like this. But you can develop these skills over time until you're writing an essay like this on your third or fourth draft, and then maybe your second. Work on these skills separately and in tandem. Never get too attached to one essay. Keep writing and practicing. You'll get your essays to this level and beyond.

There's no cookie cutter way to write a great essay. Instead, find ways to connect the great weapons you have in your arsenal. Play around with your Pillars, Archetypes, and Rhetorical Techniques. See what you come up with and then keep working at it.

Don't wait until 12th grade to start writing. Application essay questions almost never change and are usually extremely broad. The only exception is University of Chicago's essay question, which changes yearly. But even on that application, you have the option of answering a previous year's essay question, or creating your own. Give yourself a year or more to think about the essay topics.

A note for parents: applicants don't answer just one essay question. Depending on how many colleges they apply to, competitive students answer about 30-60 essay questions. It's as tough as writing a book. Would you expect your child to write a great book in a few weeks? Probably not. You'd expect it to take a year or more. Make sure that the student has the time to do this, and you'll give yourself the best chances for Ivy and Top 20 admissions.

DEBATE AND COMMUNITY ESSAYS

There are two essay question types that present more challenge to students than others. These are essays about Debate and essays about Community. Here are a few examples of essays about Debate:

- **Brown:** Brown's culture fosters a community in which students challenge the ideas of others and have their ideas challenged in return, promoting a deeper and clearer understanding of the complex issues confronting society. This active engagement in dialogue is as present outside the classroom as it is in academic spaces. Tell us about a time you were challenged by a perspective that differed from your own. How did you respond?
- **Princeton:** At Princeton, we value diverse perspectives and the ability to have respectful dialogue about difficult issues. Share a time when you had a conversation with a person or a group of people about a difficult topic. What insight did you gain, and how would you incorporate that knowledge into your thinking in the future?
- **Duke:** We believe there is benefit in sharing and sometimes questioning our beliefs or values; who do you agree with on the big important things, or who do you have your most interesting disagreements with? What are you agreeing or disagreeing about?

Most students have no idea what to do with these questions. Usually, students write an essay about having their eyes opened to a well-known progressive viewpoint. For example, the student might write about having his eyes opened to racial struggles, gender identity issues, and the like.

Those essays sound like pandering while simultaneously sounding ignorant. The student's big intellectual discovery is something commonly known by literally millions of people. The essay falls flat and the student gets rejected.

Essays about intellectual debates should be part of your Heroic journey into Uncharted Territory. You have two options:

- The debate can push you from Charted Territory into Uncharted Territory.
- The debate can be in Uncharted Territory the whole time.

Remember that Uncharted Territory involves ideas that are previously unknown to the human race. Moving from one common view to another is not moving into Uncharted Territory.

All Liberal views are Charted. So are all Conservative views. Only brand new views, new analyses, and totally new perspectives are Uncharted.

The ideal way to write the Debate essays is to engage in actual intellectual discussions and debates. You can try debating with your friends and family. If they are unwilling to debate intellectual topics, just turn to the Internet. Someone on Reddit, a social media site, or the comment section of a newspaper article will happily debate you.

But not all debates go into Uncharted Territory. Most just involve each side repeating their talking points. To push a debate into Uncharted Territory, you will need to do two things. First, you will need to listen to and carefully consider the opposing view. Second, you will need to do research. Find studies that support or oppose your view. Do the same with philosophical arguments: try to understand both the ones that support your view and the ones that oppose it. Keep patiently listening, researching, and debating until you or your debating opponent stumble into Uncharted Territory, and then keep going.

If you're already in Uncharted Territory and working with people who are in the same region of Uncharted Territory, many of your normal conversations will include the kinds of Uncharted Debates you can use. Many of the new ideas in this book, for example, grew out of debates between the two authors.

Many students attempt to just make up the debate story. Doing so is extremely difficult. It takes much more work to invent a debate than to just have an actual debate on the Internet. However, it can be done successfully. If you want to go that route, here are a few tips on how to use creative writing to invent a debate that goes into Uncharted Territory.

Make your opponent the opposite of a stereotype. Essentially, do a Reversal. If your opponent is in favor of legalizing all guns, don't make him an ex-sniper. Make him a Buddhist monk. Try to make the opponent the last person you would expect to have that view.

If he's pro-life, make him an abortion doctor. If he wants to raise taxes, make him a self-made millionaire. If he wants to lower taxes, make him an IRS agent. Do the opposite of the expected.

Debate like a chess master. Chess grandmasters often play both sides of the game, alternating between playing black and white. They do their best to help each side defeat the other. When they play white, they are trying to make white win. When they switch sides, they are doing their absolute best to make black win. They don't play one side poorly; they play both sides as well as they possibly can.

Debate like that. Give the best argument you can for one side. Then come up with the best argument you can for the other side. Keep doing that until you find yourself in Uncharted Territory.

The more specific your topic is, the better. A debate about the growth of a specific type of algae will be stronger than a general debate about the environment.

Research both sides of the debate thoroughly when coming up with arguments. Writing a fictional debate that works usually takes several weeks of research, writing, and thinking.

The other big essays that stump students are essays about Community. Here are a few examples:

- **Columbia:** A hallmark of the Columbia experience is being able to learn and thrive in an equitable and inclusive community with a wide range of perspectives. Tell us about an aspect of your own perspective, viewpoint or lived experience that is important to you, and describe how it has shaped the way you would learn from and contribute to Columbia's diverse and collaborative community.
- **Cornell Engineering:** Diversity in all forms is intrinsic to excellence in engineering. Engineering the best solutions to complex problems is often achieved by drawing from the diverse ingenuity of people from different backgrounds, lived experiences, and identities. How do you see yourself contributing to the diversity and/or the inclusion of the Cornell Engineering community? What is the unique voice you would bring to the Cornell Engineering community?
- **UPenn:** How will you explore the community at Penn? Consider how Penn will help shape your perspective and identity, and how your identity and perspective will help shape Penn.
- **Duke:** We seek a diverse student body that embodies the wide range of human experience. In that context, we are interested in what you'd like to share about your lived experiences and how they've influenced how you think of yourself.
- **Tufts:** How have the environments or experiences of your upbringing—your family, home, neighborhood, or community—shaped the person you are today?

- **Swarthmore:** Swarthmore students' worldviews are often forged by their prior experiences and exposure to ideas and values. Our students are often mentored, supported, and developed by their immediate context—in their neighborhoods, communities of faith, families, and classrooms. Reflect on what elements of your home, school, or community have shaped you or positively impacted you. How have you grown or changed because of the influence of your community?

It may seem impossible to make these essays be rare enough. No matter what your race is, several million other students have the same race. Millions of other students have the same religion as you. Millions of other students will share any demographic element you choose.

One way to make these essays work is to define your community around one or more of your Pillars. For example, if your Activity for Fun involves making floating toys, then your community can be the Community of Toy Innovators. If your Intellectual Mission Statement involves studying ancient Peloponnesian humor, then your community can be People Who Study Humor. Note that your community will be slightly more general than the associated Pillar, but it is not broad enough to include millions of people.

Once you have the community, then use Archetypes to describe your role in that community. You can use the Adult Hero archetype to describe yourself as a maverick or iconoclast in that community. You might be a renegade in the Toy Innovator Community.

You can also use the Nerd archetype and talk about how you focus on the minor things others don't think matter. For example, you might talk about how you focus on things others ignore in the Humor Analyst Community.

Almost all of these essays should include a depiction of your Heroic Persistence and exploration of Uncharted Territory.

Building a community around one of your Pillars and then using the Archetypes to define your role within that community can create essays that will help you stand out and get in.

7

AN ADVANCED TECHNIQUE

This book has focused on the basic techniques of Ivy strategy and is designed for those new to these ideas.

However, there is a limitless number of advanced and nuanced techniques you can use to get an edge over your competition. This section will examine one of those techniques. This section is advanced; if you find it too strange, difficult, or confusing, just go to the next section.

This technique involves influencing the physical state of an application reader in order to make him view your application more favorably.

We'll start with a handy tool called "The Map of Consciousness," which was developed by psychologist and doctor David R. Hawkins. It has been used by countless people to improve their psychological health, fight depression and anxiety, change their worldview, and transform their lives.

It can also be used to write incredibly powerful college essays that influence the gut instincts of application readers.

The map is on the next page:

Level	Energetic "Frequency"	Associated Emotional State
Enlightenment	700-1000	Ineffable
Peace	600	Bliss
Joy	540	Serenity
Love	500	Reverence
Reason	400	Understanding
Acceptance	350	Forgiveness
Willingness	310	Optimism
Neutrality	250	Trust
Courage	200	Affirmation
Pride	175	Scorn
Anger	150	Hate
Desire	125	Craving
Fear	100	Anxiety
Grief	75	Regret
Apathy	50	Despair
Guilt	30	Blame
Shame	20	Humiliation

You may have learned in English classes that great characters in literature have "character development." The Map of Consciousness can help make sure that the character in your essay (yourself), has the right kind of character development.

Good character development moves up the Map of Consciousness. Bad character development moves down. A change of opinion without any motion up or down the map is just a lack of character development.

Colleges ask you about experiences that changed your perspectives. Too often, students create perspective changes that don't move up the map, but rather stay in the same place.

Consider this example answer:

> "When I was younger, I thought that all guns should be banned, and everyone who disagreed was an idiot. Then, I realized that all guns should be legalized, and everyone who disagrees is an idiot."

This essay starts out at the level of Pride (as shown by the scorn it embodies), and it also ends at the level of Pride.

For college strategy, Courage and higher are the "good" levels, and Pride and lower are the "bad" levels. If you're writing an essay about character development, your ending point should be at the level of Courage or higher.

In an ideal world, everyone would gradually progress up the map through their lives. But the sad reality is that the opposite often happens. You may have heard adults around you saying something like this:

> "When I was a kid, I thought the world was full of just fun and cool stuff and excitement. But then I grew up, and realized that in the real world, you just need to keep your head down, shut up, and work, and if you don't work well, you're worthless."

This is a mild exaggeration, but the world is full of precisely this kind of pessimism masquerading as wisdom.

Using the Map of Consciousness to analyze this, we can see that the person starts out at the level of Joy and ends at the level of Shame.

That attitude has become the unfortunate definition of "maturity," and the common portrayal of "the real world" has become a vaguely bureaucratic nightmare. With this "guidance" from the adults around them, many well-meaning students write essays in which they start out full of optimism and end up full of guilt and shame.

Great college essays do the opposite: they convincingly move up the Map instead of plummeting to the bottom.

To do that convincingly, you'll need to do more than say, "I started out apathetic, but then I was full of willingness." That's unlikely to convince anyone.

Instead, you'll use the ultimate secret to outsmarting a personality test.

How to Outsmart a Personality Test

To outsmart any personality test, use this quote:

> "We don't see the world as the world is. We see the world as we are."

You may be scratching your head at that. How can what we see possibly be affected by our personality?

Imagine that you ask someone to describe their desk and they give you this insane response:

> My desk is great. I have a pen at the desk, and it's great because if you get into a fight, you can stab someone in the neck with it. Also, I have a cell phone charging cord, which is awesome because you can use it to strangle someone if you're attacked. I usually keep a water cup at the desk, and that's a great tool to bludgeon someone if you're in a fight.

What that person described is probably technically true. But the violence, rage, and fear in that description reveals everything about the person's personality and rather little about the desk!

If anyone describes anything, she will invariably reveal parts of her personality. You can try this yourself. Ask someone you know well to describe something. It could be their room. It could be the floor. It could be the car in front of them. It could be literally anything. Listen carefully; you'll be surprised by how much of their personality they inadvertently reveal.

Any object, place, or idea works for this. In fact, having someone describe a smudge of ink on a page can reveal a lot about their personality. In the famed Rorschach test, subjects describe what they see in an inkblot. Their descriptions reveal plenty about their personality. But that's not because those inkblots are magic; having someone describe anything at all will reveal aspects of their personality.

Dr. David Hawkins, who developed the Map of Consciousness, illustrates this principle with an example in his book *Power vs. Force*:

> Imagine a so-called "bum" on a street corner: In a fashionable neighborhood in a big city stands an old man in tattered clothes, alone, leaning against the corner of an elegant brownstone.
>
> Look at him from the perspective of various levels of consciousness and note the differences in how he appears. From the bottom of the scale, at a level of 20 (Shame), the bum is dirty, disgusting, and disgraceful. From level 30 (Guilt), he would be blamed for his condition. He deserves what he gets; he is probably a lazy welfare cheat. At 50 (Hopelessness), his plight might appear desperate, evidence that society cannot do anything about homelessness. At 75 (Grief), the old man looks tragic, friendless, and forlorn.
>
> At a consciousness level of 100 (Fear), we might see the bum as threatening, a social menace. Perhaps we should call the police before he commits some crime. At 125 (Desire), he might represent a frustrating problem—why does somebody not do something? At 150 (Anger), the old man might look like he could be violent; or, on the other hand, one could be furious that such a condition

exists. At 175 (Pride), he could be seen as an embarrassment or as lacking the self-respect to better himself.

At 200 (Courage), we might be motivated to wonder if there is a local homeless shelter; all he needs is a job and a place to live. At 250 (Neutrality), the bum looks okay, maybe even interesting. "Live and let live," we might say; after all, he is not hurting anyone. At 310 (Willingness), we might decide to go down there and see what we can do to cheer him up, or volunteer some time at the local mission.

At 350 (Acceptance), the man on the corner appears intriguing. He probably has an interesting story to tell; he is where he is for reasons we may never understand. At 400 (Reason), he is a symptom of the current economic and social malaise, or perhaps a good subject for an in-depth psychological study, worthy of a government grant.

At the higher levels, the old man begins to look not only interesting, but friendly and even lovable. Perhaps we would then be able to see that he was, in fact, one who had transcended social limits and gone free, a joyful old guy with the wisdom of age in his face and the serenity that comes from indifference to material things. At level 600 (Peace), he is revealed as our own inner self in its temporary expression.

When approached, the bum's response to these different levels of consciousness would also vary. With some people, he would feel secure, with others, frightened or dejected. Some would make him angry, and others would delight him. Some people he would therefore avoid, and others greet with pleasure. (Thus it is said that what we meet is actually a mirror.)

The way we describe things other than ourselves reveals a lot about ourselves. That's a major reason that colleges ask seemingly nonsensical questions. When they ask you about your favorite keepsake, or something that inspires you, or your favorite word, they're asking you to describe something else so that they can catch a glimpse of your true personality.

Let's look at excerpts from a famous successful Harvard essay (the full text can easily be found with an internet search). In this essay, the author masterfully shows his transformation. Using the Map of Consciousness, we can see how he first moves down the map, and then up the map to an unusually high level.

The scene describes the national finals of a Scrabble tournament. Although it only covers a few minutes, it beautifully portrays powerful character development. In this scene, the author is playing against Frank Lee, his final opponent.

At the beginning, the author is winning. On the map, he's hovering around Courage or Pride:

> …The clock is ticking down, 37, 36, 35, and soon Frank utters a mammoth sigh and places his S next to the U of "URIC," forming "US." I smile; Frank is almost definitely going to play "OWNS" or "WINOS" and I will handily win the game…

But then, things go poorly. Frank uses an amazing word and wins. The author plummets into Shame:

> My jaw drops almost to table level. Frank had used all of his letters at once, thereby getting a 50-point bonus to his score. He wins the game 425-392. The perfect irony of the situation… the perfect irony of the word itself! I had arrogantly thought that I was the one who would be celebrating, but humble Frank Lee is the one

who remains standing (sitting) with the single word that would 'live forever' in my mind.

My head hits the table, one of the ubiquitous pieces of folding plastic that dominate the room. How could I be so idiotic? How could I make such a critical mistake? How, how how?...

But then, something amazing happens: with an encouraging word from his competitor, the author skyrockets into Acceptance and then Love.

… But as I sit, silently berating myself to no end, Frank looks up at me and says, "I take no pleasure in that win Christopher."

I slowly lift my head to see his weathered blue eyes looking genuinely back at mine. He pauses, and it seems to me as though the whole room had gone silent. He looks at me more sincerely than ever before, an impenetrable, wholehearted gaze into my eyes. "I hope you can leave knowing that you've come away from this tournament with a better prize than anyone could have given you Christopher, because you deserve to be happy, and you deserve to be happy with what you've become."

The words, the points, and the money all disappear. I look around the room and realize that I am not surrounded by diehard competitors who play this odd game for fame and glory, but by people just like me who had wanted to join this eccentric subculture, who had wanted to finally be accepted in their lives. For us, Scrabble is not about satisfying a vain addiction to competition, but rather about the heartfelt players like Frank Lee who have come together to support one another and their love for the game, foibles and all. I am not playing this game for dollars and cents; I am playing it for a sense of family.

Across the table is not just a man with a striped hat, an oxygen tank, and orange diabetic footsoles; this is a man who had been taken under the wing of our minuscule clique of players and accepted just the way he is: as a lover of language and a man of honor. Good game, Frank.

That level of movement on the Map of Consciousness is incredible. Few novels have that kind of character growth; the author of this essay does it in just a page. Courage to Shame to Acceptance to Love is a powerful journey.

Using the Map of Consciousness isn't as hard as you might think. Here are some rules.

1. Don't use the words on the map. It's fine to show Courage, but don't use the word "courage."
2. Describe something other than yourself (like your Scrabble championship opponent or the room you're sitting in) so the reader can "figure out" your personality independently.
3. You should end up higher than you started, but it's okay to go downwards in the middle.

Our final bit of advice: beware of Pride and its associated emotion Scorn. The entire Ivy application process embodies Pride. Not surprisingly, most students radiate scornful pride throughout their essays. The Pride-based application process magnetically draws Pride-based essays. Pride remains in the "negative" side of things. Great applications always show levels higher than Pride.

The key to outsmarting any personality test, including an Ivy application, is to remember that how you describe the world reveals more about yourself than about the world. As Ralph Waldo Emerson put it,

"People do not seem to realize that their opinion of the world is also a confession of character." By adjusting the way you describe the world, you adjust the way application readers see your personality.

A FEW COMMON PERSONALITY TEST QUESTIONS

Your English teachers have probably advised you, "Show, don't tell." That's great advice. Let the reader figure out who you are, and they will believe their conclusions.

We often tell our students, "No one trusts anyone, but everyone trusts themselves." If you tell a college that you're creative, they probably won't believe you. But if the admissions officer figures out on his own that you are creative, he will believe his own conclusion. We all trust our own wisdom completely.

The philosopher Thomas Hobbes describes our tendency to trust our own wisdom:

> "For such is the nature of men that howsoever they may acknowledge many others to be more witty, or more eloquent or more learned, yet they will hardly believe there be many so wise as themselves; for they see their own wit at hand, and other men's at a distance."

We can use this principle to illustrate how we can easily answer essay or interview questions in a way that causes the admissions officer or interviewer to come to controllable conclusions.

One common question type asks what historical figure you would like to meet, and what you would ask them. Depending on how you answer this question, you might come across as anything from someone interested in politics or plants to a sociopath interested in money and fame.

Let's try to showcase an interest in politics and political philosophy. But don't choose someone like Abraham Lincoln or George Washington. That won't convey an interest in politics; it will only tell the listener that we want him to **believe** that we're interested in politics.

Instead, let's choose a scientist. We can pick Dr. Jonas Salk, the creator of the polio vaccine, and then ask him a political question.

"I would ask Dr. Salk about his views on mandatory vaccination. For example, does he believe that we have a moral responsibility to get vaccinated to create herd immunity to protect the immunocompromised? Does he believe that parents can morally vaccinate their children to protect others, not necessarily to protect the child?"

Someone who asks a scientist a political question is radiating an interest in political thought. An interviewer who hears that answer comes to the conclusion, on his own, that the student is interested in political thought, and then he trusts his own conclusion.

Note that we didn't ask a scientist a scientific question. An interviewer who hears that doesn't come to any special conclusion. He doesn't figure anything out, so there's no conclusion he can come to and then trust absolutely.

By asking an expert in one area a surprising question about a second area, you show a strong interest in the second area. For example, asking Einstein a question about fashion shows interest in fashion. Asking Voltaire a question about desserts shows an interest in dessert. The listener deduces your interests, and then believes that conclusion because she arrived at it herself.

We can also use this principle (people trust only themselves) to help you get the most out of your Activity for Fun on your application. In fact, even if you're a senior who doesn't have time to create a great Activity for Fun, you can use this principle to get the most out of a common activity.

Specifically, we can use this technique to answer questions like, "What do you do for fun?" or "What brings you joy?"

We'll start by picking a character trait to convey. Let's try "creativity."

At this point, most people make the same mistake. They pick a highly obvious way to show creativity. For example, they might talk about their interest in painting or pottery:

> "I love painting for fun. With painting, I can express my creativity. I can use the paints to create different images and patterns, as well as express my emotions."

The problem with that is it doesn't make the reader make any connections. The reader doesn't come to an independent conclusion. It looks like a passionless lie. If someone was entirely uninterested in creativity, but wanted to convince someone he was creative, he would write something like that.

The applicant hopes that the reader will trust him. But no application reader will blindly trust a student. Application readers trust their own judgment and their own, independent conclusions. They trust themselves. To make them believe something about your personality, you need to make them come to a conclusion on their own.

Let's create a better answer to showcase creativity. We start by thinking of things that are inherently uncreative. Doing the dishes, doing pushups, running, and brushing teeth come to mind. Any could work well. We'll choose "doing push-ups" as the activity.

Our goal is to make the reader come to the conclusion that we are creative. We won't use the word creative ever. We want the reader to "figure out" that we're creative, and then trust her own analysis.

> "I love doing push-ups. I enjoy coming up with different angles, different hand grips, and various MacGyvered equipment. I've made a kind of modified version of gymnastics rings that I use for decline pushups, as well as stands for my feet that allows much finer adjustments than normal equipment."

Note that this is infinitely more believable and interesting. Even though the answer never uses the word "creativity," the application reader would inevitably come to the conclusion that the writer brought creative thought into every part of his life. After all, if someone is creative when doing push-ups, that person is probably creative with everything. If you're creative with the least inherently creative thing on earth, you're probably going to be more creative with everything else.

The key is to lay out the pieces that will guide the reader to a predictable conclusion.

Here's what works:

1. You give the reader enough information to come up with her own conclusion.
2. The reader then trusts her own conclusion completely.

Note that the reader isn't trusting you. She's trusting herself.
Here's what doesn't work.

1. You present a case directly to the reader, hoping that the reader will trust you.

Millions of people are willing to lie to get into Harvard. Almost everyone lies on their application to some extent. Harvard's job is is to catch those lies. They're pretty good at it.

A Harvard application reader won't trust you. But she will trust her own conclusions. By shaping those conclusions, you can control the reader's beliefs.

8

LOGISTICS AND TIMELINES

This section looks at some time sensitive parts of the Ivy application process.

THE PRINCETON PAPER

Princeton requires each student to submit a graded English paper from school as part of his or her application. The writing style of that paper should match the writing style of your application essays.

If they don't match, it may appear that someone else wrote your application essay, which can cause you to get rejected. On the other hand, if your Princeton application essay looks like the essays that most straight A students write in school English classes, then you will definitely get rejected. The writing level of a successful Ivy essay is far beyond the writing level needed to get A's in school English classes.

The solution is to start building your writing skills to the Ivy application level in 9th grade or earlier. Specifically, you should start including Categorizations, Reversals, and Analogical Reasoning in your school English papers. Strive to make your English papers truly exceptional.

By the time you apply to Princeton, you should have several amazing English papers to choose from.

The grades on those papers won't matter; only the quality of the thought and insights will. A brilliant paper that gets a C will beat a low-quality paper that gets an A. The application reader will read your paper and come to an independent judgment.

THE SAT AND PSAT

You can take the SAT as many times as you want. Elite colleges usually use a "superscore," which is created by taking your highest verbal score from all of your SATs and adding it to the highest math score from all of your SATs. The math score from one test can be added to the verbal score of another test.

It doesn't matter how many times you take the SAT. Whether you take it three times or thirty, only the highest scores matter.

A common fear is that if you take the SAT too many times, the application reader will look unfavorably on your score. This is a myth. Application readers do not waste their time micro-analyzing your scores. Instead, they look at your essays, extracurriculars, and recommendation letters.

A computer can look at your SAT score. In fact, computers usually do. The limited time of highly overworked application readers goes entirely toward analyzing your essays, recommendation letters, and extracurriculars.

The PSAT, on the other hand, is quite different. Only one PSAT counts. That's the one you take in October of 11th grade. That test, and only that test, determines whether you get into the National Merit program. You must have a high enough 11th grade PSAT score to become a National Merit semifinalist, and you only have one chance.

PSATs taken in 9th and 10th grade have zero importance. Only the 11th grade test matters.

You have one shot at getting a high PSAT score that counts, but many shots at getting a high SAT score that counts. Thus, the best strategy is to take the SAT before the PSAT. Use the SAT as practice. You should take your first real, official SAT in 10th grade. You may need to take it more than once in 10th grade to get your desired score. If you can get a high enough score on the SAT, then you can get a high enough score on the PSAT. The PSAT covers very similar material and is a little bit easier.

This is the opposite of what most people do. Most people use the PSAT as practice for the SAT. That's a terrible idea. The SAT can be retaken multiple times; the PSAT can't. Make the SAT the warmup and the PSAT the championship to get an advantage over your competition.

THE COLLEGE COUNSELOR QUESTIONNAIRE

At some point, usually during 11th grade, you and your parents will get a questionnaire from your school's college counselor questionnaire. It may be a paper form, or it may be presented using the Naviance system.

That questionnaire is the single most powerful tool in Ivy Strategy.

The simple fact is that Ivies don't really trust you. To them, you're just another student who will say literally anything to get in. However, they trust your college counselor completely. Here's why: if your college counselor ever lies to them, they can, and will, retaliate against your school. If your college counselor lies to Harvard, no one from your school is getting into Harvard for about the next century. Schools know that. College counselors know that. So, they never lie, and Ivies believe them 100%.

But college counselors rarely know any of the students at their schools. Thus, to create their official recommendation, they mostly copy and paste from your answers on your college counselor questionnaire.

In fact, some of these questionnaires will blatantly ask you something along the lines of, "If you were going to write the first paragraph of your recommendation, what would you write?" That's a pretty obvious way of letting you know that they'll be copying directly from your questionnaire.

The college counselor questionnaire transforms your distrusted statements into absolute gospel, like Rumpelstiltskin spinning straw into gold. That makes the college counselor questionnaire one of the most valuable tools in Ivy Strategy.

Your questionnaire should focus on your Four Pillars and nothing else. Make sure every question connects to the Four Pillars.

Let's say you get the question, "What's your favorite class at school?" You might say, "I really liked American History because that's where I first got interested in the History of Carrots," or "I really like American History because that's where I was inspired to make video games about dogs."

Every single answer should focus on one of your Four Pillars. The same is true for your parents' answers on their questionnaires.

You should not write about anything other than your Four Pillars on your college counselor questionnaires. Here's why:

Suppose there are 200 questions. You answer 199 of those questions with answers about the tree jewelry you're making and the book you're writing about carrots. However, you answer one question by discussing a super common extracurricular (e.g., Model U.N., Relay for Life, running charity bake sales).

Your college counselor probably hasn't read this book. He might not have great instincts. He might not know much about Ivy League culture. Trying to help you, he might unstrategically focus on Debate Club or All State Choir instead of the book about carrots. He thinks the book about carrots might not be that important since few people are interested in carrots. But Debate Club is well-respected resume padding. You know that the Ivy League isn't looking for resume padding, but your college counselor might not. In trying to help you, he might accidentally sink your application.

This happens far more often than you'd hope. Inexperienced college counselors routinely make the mistake of emphasizing sports, clubs, and community service at retirement homes. Give your counselor no option other than to write about your Four Pillars.

This technique is common in politics, by the way. When political leaders are interviewed by reporters, they know that the reporter must use a quote. Suppose the political leader wants to get in a quote about ending the sales tax, but the reporter doesn't want that. If the political leader says, "I want to end the sales tax," as an answer to every single question, the reporter is forced to put that quote in the paper. But if the politician says,

"I want to end the sales tax" 1,000 times, and "I like dogs" one time, the reporter can use the dog quote instead.

Don't let your counselor water down your message. He should know about your Four Pillars and nothing else.

FAQS

Are College Visits Important?

You have probably realized that showing interest in a college can help you get into the college. One common way to show interest in a college is to visit the college, hoping that visiting the college will increase your chances of getting in.

That doesn't work. First, it's far too common to work. Any common approach to anything at all in Ivy strategy doesn't work. Rare things work. Nothing else does.

Second, it would be utterly impossible for college visits to confer any advantage in today's political climate. Imagine a single mom in Detroit working three jobs, who is too busy to fly her son to visit Stanford. Do you think Stanford would hold that against that student, or confer an advantage to other students over that student because they visited? Of course not.

Showing interest in a college is a great idea, but visiting the college isn't the way to do it. The best way to show interest in a college is to discuss the research of a specific professor from the college to which you are applying. Keeping the Adult Hero archetype in mind, find clever and compelling ways to disagree with that professor somewhere in your application essays. Discuss the research at the college. Research defines a college; the physical campus does not.

The right time to visit a college is after you get into multiple colleges. At that point, visiting a campus can help you decide which college you like more.

Should I take Summer Classes at an Ivy?

Many people ask whether summer programs at Ivy League colleges help you get into that college. The general rule of thumb is this: if you pay to attend the program, it won't help you get in. If it's a competitive program that either costs nothing or includes a stipend, that program can help you get in. The Research Science Institute (RSI) at MIT is an example of a cost-free program that is hard to get into. Getting into it helps your application.

There are also similar year-long and multi-year programs that can help your chances. For example, MIT PRIMES is a year-long, cost-free program that is extremely tough to get into. If you get in, it will dramatically increase your chances of getting into MIT.

On the other hand, summer courses and programs that you pay to attend at Ivies are usually just cash grabs and do not help your application at all. As mentioned earlier in this book, undergraduate students are often seen as cash cows whose tuition dollars fund graduate research. High school students are more cash cow-ish in the eyes of Ivies. If you're paying to attend a program at a competitive college, it is unlikely to help your application. To make things worse, that program will take time away from independent work that will help your application.

The same is true of programs like the Center for Talented Youth (CTY) and the Center for Bright Kids (CBK). First, far too many students do these programs. They dramatically fail in terms of rarity. They also focus on Charted Territory rather than Uncharted Territory. They focus on advanced classes rather than research. Most of the cost-free programs focus on exploring Uncharted Territory through cutting edge research.

The best summer programs in colleges, like the best things in life, are free.

Do Interviews Matter?

There's a myth out there that interviews don't matter. Obviously, that's totally false. College applications are personality tests; what could possibly be a better way to gauge an applicant's personality than an interview?

But there is a reason for this belief. Often, people whose interviews seem to go well get rejected, and those whose interviews seem to go poorly get accepted. Let's see why that happens.

Imagine you're playing basketball against a three-year-old. Would you play your heart out, or would you go easy on him? Most people would go easy on him. It would just be in poor taste to play your heart out against a kid who can barely hold onto the ball.

The same rule applies to interviews. If you're an interviewer, and the interviewee is shy, fumbling, boring, socially unskilled, and unintelligent, you're just going to be nice to the person. It's the only humane thing to do. You won't recommend that the applicant be admitted, but you'll be polite.

The interviewee may think that the interview went well. After all, the interviewer was nice. In reality, it went terribly, and the interviewer was just being decent.

On the other hand, imagine you're interviewing someone confident, insightful, brilliant, and socially adept. You might debate her a bit. You might push her, to see if she can handle it. You might intentionally disagree with her to see if she stands up for her views. You're only doing that because you see her as a real contender.

That interviewee might think the interview went terribly. After all, the interviewer was arguing with her. But the interviewer only argued because he saw the candidate as a strong contender. He probably recommended her for admission.

Interviewers are usually polite to hopelessly bad candidates, and often debate with great candidates. Thus, people who get rejected often have pleasant interviews, and people who get accepted often have confrontational interviews.

A hostile interview is usually a good sign. If your interviewer debates or challenges you, debate back. It often means he sees you as a strong candidate.

What are the minimum requirements to get into an Ivy?

Getting into an Ivy is a competitive process, much like a football game. How many points do you need to win a football game? You need one more point than the other team.

Harvard admits around 2,000 people a year. If only 1,999 applications are better than yours, you'll get in. If 2,000 applications are better than yours, you won't.

Some students confuse application requirements with what it takes to get in. Most Ivies have fairly minimal application requirements, including things like a minimum of 3 years of English and the like. Those do not tell you what it takes to win the competition to get in. Those just tell you what you need to do to be allowed to submit an application at all.

For example, at the time of this writing, Harvard and many other colleges are SAT optional. That only means you can apply without an SAT score. It doesn't mean that now high SAT scores have no value.

Most of the application is "optional." All extracurriculars are optional. Class participation in school is optional. Getting featured in the news is optional. But those things are still beneficial.

This is a competition. It's a race to be one step better than the other person. Every strategic piece helps.

Do service trips help?

Many students consider "service trips," which are community service trips to less developed countries.

Many students instinctively feel there is something "right" about service trips. Their instincts are close…but unfortunately wrong.

Service trips feel sort of Uncharted. You're going to a less developed part of the world. In other words, the destination country is itself sort of Uncharted. Intuitively, the student knows his application needs to be Uncharted, and the service trip seems close enough.

But the reality is that Service Trips are the most Charted type of community service that exists. In these trips, wealthy western students pay a lot of money to go to underdeveloped countries to have a good experience. The people who run these programs make plenty of money doing so—they make money in dollars and euros and spend it in the local currency. To them, the western students are cash cows that must be protected no matter what. They make sure that the student doesn't stray from the safe path at all.

Service trips are tightly controlled with heavy guidance. Students rarely, if ever, go into Uncharted Territory on service trips.

But it gets worse. Because of their expense, service trips are usually seen as a sign of being overprivileged. Coming across as an overprivileged student in Charted territory is a terrible mix.

You don't need to go to an undeveloped country to find Uncharted Territory. Uncharted Territory is all around you. Instead of doing a Charted activity in an undeveloped country, find real Uncharted Territory closer to home, and save a few thousand dollars at the same time.

If I do enough charted extracurriculars, would that meet the scarcity requirements?

Students often ask if by doing a large number of extracurriculars, they can meet the scarcity requirements. For example, if a student joins 700 clubs, would that be enough to meet the scarcity requirement for Ivy admissions? Would that be rare enough?

First, the number of extracurriculars would have to be staggeringly high. Each year, tens of thousands of students schedule every waking minute with one Charted extracurricular or another. Many of these students push past their physical limits to do it, including going without sufficient sleep for years at a time. Doing more Charted extracurriculars than all of these students would probably be impossible and might harm your physical health. We strongly advise against that.

But let's say you got access to a time machine and could do it. Would that make you rare enough?

Yes.

But it would fail miserably on the Archetypes and mythical side of things.

Ivy admissions officers don't count up all of your extracurriculars. In fact, the applications only have room for 10 or fewer. If you do 1,000 activities, 990 go unreported. If you attach a separate resume with a list of Charted extracurriculars (which would be a terrible idea), the admissions officer will just ignore most of it. They don't have the time to read a list of 1,000 things. Even if they had the time, they wouldn't, because it's too tediously boring, and no one wants to read a list like that.

Quality matters. Quantity does not. And the specific quality that matters is Unchartedness. Through Uncharted territory we can bring forth the Hero and the Adult Hero archetypes.

A thousand fools do not equal a wise man, and a thousand Charted extracurriculars do not equal one Uncharted extracurricular. A small number of unique, Uncharted extracurriculars will always beat a large number of Charted extracurriculars.

Should I Attach a Resume?

Many colleges give you the option to attach a resume to your application. This allows you to list additional extracurriculars and work experiences.

We strongly advise that your resume contain six things and six things only: your Four Pillars, and then your two most treasured Charted activities. The Four Pillars should be listed above the Charted activities, no matter how prestigious those Charted activities are.

Let's understand why. Suppose you are the editor of your school's newspaper and the author of a book about animal hooves. If you put the school newspaper above the book, the reader sees the book as being less valuable than being the newspaper editor. On the other hand, if you put the book above being a newspaper editor, then the book is perceived as more valuable.

The value of being the school newspaper editor is already known since it's Charted. You can't increase or decrease its perceived value. The value of the Uncharted book, on the other hand, is entirely unknown. The application reader only knows its value based on how you present it. Thus, you can increase its perceived value by ranking it higher than the Charted activity (school newspaper).

If school newspaper has a value of 20, and you put the book above it, then the book gets a value of 21 or higher. If you put the book below the newspaper, then the book gets a value of 19 or lower. The value of the newspaper cannot change since it is Charted. But you get to control the perceived importance of your Uncharted activities.

This is the most important task of the resume. It's not about creating a list; it's about creating a clear ranking of significance for your Uncharted activities.

Is Homeschooling a Good Idea?

A well designed homeschool program can help you get academically ahead of your competition while also ensuring that you'll have more unstructured time to explore and develop your Four Pillars. A homeschool program entirely focused on education, self-improvement, and personal growth will enjoy a significant advantage over any other type of education. Many of our homeschool students are academically years ahead of their competition in private and magnet schools.

Aggregate homeschool data doesn't reflect this simply because many families choose homeschooling for non-academic reasons. Millions homeschool for religious reasons or as part of a hippie ideal. Students in that type of homeschooling don't have any particular advantage for Ivy admissions.

However, academically competitive suburban families that choose homeschooling frequently end up light years ahead of their competition in both academics and in the rarity, completeness, and quantity of their Pillars.

You're not limited to just Four Pillars. You can have several Activities for Service, several Intellectual Mission Statements, several things you do for fun. Most public- and private-schooled students don't have time for any more than four. Homeschooled students do.

Is an Ivy Education Worth It?

This question is really several questions.

The first question is, "Is a college education better than an education you can get outside of college?" Absolutely not. Through self-study, reading research from Ivy professors, using programs like MIT's OpenCourseWare, Open Yale Courses, and MasterClass, you can get an education far superior to anything you can get in an Ivy League college. We're living in an Information Age, where elite information is no longer hidden behind university walls.

The next question is, "Is a college degree necessary?" At the moment, most medical schools and law schools require that applicants have an undergraduate degree. In those areas, a degree is necessary. Outside of those areas, it isn't, and is becoming less and less so as more businesses switch over to skills testing and behavioral evaluations.

The final question is, "Is an Ivy League degree prestigious?" Yes, of course. An Ivy degree is like a Rolex watch. It might not have any practical function ($10 watches are more accurate), but it does convey social prestige effectively.

What if I Get Into an Ivy, But the Work is Too Hard?

Ivy League colleges are extremely hard to get into, but the workload is comparatively easy once you're there. Getting in is, by far, the hardest part.

NEXT STEPS

You now know the secret codes of college strategy. You know about the Four Pillars: Activity for Fun, Activity for Service, Intellectual Pursuit for Fun, and Intellectual Mission Statement. You know about the Hero, the Nerd, and the Adult Hero. You know about Reversals, Categorizations, and Analogical Reasoning. You know about the Map of Consciousness and how to use it to create amazing essays.

Armed with this new perspective, it might be a good time to review other "famous" essays and see how you can better understand them. One of our favorite books on the subject is *Essays that Worked for College Applications*, by Curry, Kasbar, and Baer.

Read through some of those essays and see if you can identify the Hero, the Nerd, and the Adult Hero. See if they use Categorizations or Analogies. See if they Reverse things or disagree with prompts or Guides.

The book series *50 Successful Harvard Essays* is another great source. Note that some of those essays are a lot better than others. If you're Asian or you live in a competitive metro area (New York, DC, or Boston) your essays need to match the best ones in the book. If you're from Idaho and you're not Asian, use any of those you like as a benchmark.

You can also look for these archetypes and techniques everywhere else—movies, music, politics, philosophy. These techniques and archetypes aren't limited to college essays; they bring phenomenal success in other areas as well. Make the world your source of study for these powerful tactics so you can master them and apply them in your college strategy.

Finally, make sure you check out the free, online video courses at www.InvitationtotheIvies.com. Current courses include an introduction to Ivy Strategy, which can help reinforce some of what you've learned in this book, and a course about college interviews, which has information not included in this book. You can also find information there about how to get individualized help with your own Ivy strategy, Ivy essays, and Ivy interviews.

The final note is for other college strategists. We hope some of the ideas and research in this book will help you help your students. We also offer a "second set of eyes" service for college essays. Chelsey and Arvin turn to each other for second opinions about essay drafts. If you're a solo practitioner, we're available to provide that for you as well.

ABOUT THE AUTHORS

ARVIN VOHRA

Arvin Vohra has two beliefs: hard work should always pay off, and laziness should never pay off. He wrote *Invitation to the Ivies* to show hard working, ambitious students how to defeat their lazier competition.

His company, Vohra Method, helps ambitious students dominate their academic competition, get top 1% SAT scores, and get into Ivy League colleges.

He is also the author of *The Equation for Excellence: How to Make Your Child Excel at Math*.

CHELSEY SNYDER-SINGH

Chelsey Snyder-Singh knows that ambitious students can achieve amazing things before college, and those amazing things lead to Ivy admissions. She has helped students write books, create incredible projects, design and market inventions, and get into Ivies.

She wrote *Invitation to the Ivies* to show students a path to excellence that transcends anything found in common extracurriculars.

She is also the author of *The Three-Week SAT Crash Course* book series.

From the co-author of *Invitation to the Ivies*

Three-Week Crash Course SAT

Reading

Chelsey M. Snyder

Improve your SAT score a lot. Fast.
An easy-to-read guide. NOT a textbook.

www.ingramcontent.com/pod-product-compliance
Lightning Source LLC
Chambersburg PA
CBHW020225170426
43201CB00007B/325